Lessons from the Finish Line

12 Things I Learned About Life From Running 12 Races in 12 Months

ELLEN MARRS

ISBN: 978-1516881628

Printed in the United States of America

Lessons from the Finish Line by Ellen Marrs

Cover design and layout by Brian Ring | brianringdesign@tumblr.com

Warning – Disclaimer

This book is dedicated to...

God for making ALL things possible.

Rick for being the most incredibly patient, loving
and supportive man I know. You are God's gift
to me and I am truly blessed to be your wife.

Graesen, Peyton, Michael, Rosemarie, Bella,
Annette and Jaeden for being the inspiration and
motivation behind everything I do to finish the race strong.

You are the laughter and sunshine in my days and
living proof of God's great love for me.

"Feeling gratitude and not expressing it is like wrapping a present and not giving it."

-William Arthur Ward

Acknowledgments

I Am Grateful…

To Anthony for knowing that I was a runner, before I believed it myself. Thanks for inspiring me to complete my first of many races.

To Barbara Starley for your patience, wisdom, enthusiasm and constant encouragement. God has used you in mighty ways to influence my life and write my family's story.

To Kody Bateman for teaching me the power of the "I Am" statement and for helping me to dream big again. Thanks to you and Jodi for pursuing your own dreams so that others could do the same.

To Jordan Adler for sharing your wisdom and experience with me. You are a genuine leader and I am thankful for your example to follow. You are an inspiration in business and in life.

To Jeff Packard for challenging me to express my heartfelt gratitude and bless others in the process.

To Vanessa Hunter for encouraging women to excel in the network marketing industry and support one another along the way. Your enthusiasm for what we do is contagious.

To Steve Schulz for bringing your boundless energy and excitement to every event. You make it FUN to be a part of this profession.

To Faith Herrera for knowing all my faults, fears and failures, but loving me just the same. Thank you for being beside me for all of life's biggest moments such as my wedding, the births of my children and the adoption of my "littles".

To Mandy Curtis for giving me the extra push that I needed to run my first half marathon. You are an inspiration to me and countless others. Thanks for always finding a way to make me laugh.

To Betty Pearce for your generosity and contribution to my race challenge. Thank you for providing the "book ends" for traveling to my first and last races.

To Rachel for sacrificing your own race time to encourage and accompany me to the finish line.

To Lorin for keeping an eye out for me in race #10 and ensuring that I didn't get lost along the way. Thanks for the ice cubes!

To Cynthia Hanna for your ongoing motivation, no-nonsense encouragement and willingness to share the joy (and pain) of running with me.

To Gwen Hanna for caring enough to meet me at the finish line, even when you were in the midst of your own personal challenge.

To Dr. Mike Collins for keeping me on course and moving toward my goals, physically and emotionally. You are a true caregiver, in every sense of the word.

To Dr. Eric Hazelrigg, Raquel and the entire staff at Comprehensive Women's Healthcare for taking such great care of me during each of my pregnancies.

To Laura Marra, Branden and Logan for making every adventure a fun one. Your laughter and smiles continue to bless me, in spite of the miles between us.

To Scott and Vicki Delaney for loving our family for more than a decade and showing you care in such tangible ways. Thanks for "carb loading" with us before the first race of my challenge.

To Justin Anderson for sharing your love and vision for the church in San Francisco. Thanks for allowing us to be a small part of it.

To Jason Croniser for sharing your running knowledge and for permanently loaning me the "lucky shirt".

To Mandi Croniser for teaching me a wealth of knowledge regarding natural remedies, good nutrition and anything else that may have come up in our conversations. I miss being able to walk down the street to see you.

To Monica Moraila for making sure that I was able to relax and recover after pushing my body to endure so many miles.

To Kari Peterson for being a true friend and brave soul as you cared for our children while I was traveling for my races.

To Luz Marrs for taking care of Rick and our kiddos in my absence.

To Alex Thornburg, Rylie and Reagan Howey for giving me time to write while you loved and cared for my seven Marrs munchkins. The date nights were great too!

To Renee Clark for giving me a place to hang my hardware. Thanks for your creativity and generosity in making my race boards.

To Gene and Lubeth Eller for giving me a second chance for a family when no one else would.

To Teresa Jaworski for being my big sister and showing me what true courage and genuine faith looks like. You inspire me!

To Nancy Robbins for believing that I was an author over a decade before I ever wrote the first page of this book.

To Leann McFalls for being my virtual running partner. I'm truly grateful for how God brought us together and formed such a fantastic friendship. You are a treasure and blessing in my life.

To Jill Brown for being the best first impression I could have ever had when I started in network marketing. Thank you for answering my endless list of questions at my first convention. You left your precious fingerprints on my life as you helped me to grow and learn about my company and its business model.

To Brenda Sanchez for being my cheerleader and supporter from a distance. I am still amazed at how well you were able to keep track of my races during the challenge. I appreciate you for all the ways that you have loved and encouraged me since we first met in the San Diego "party van".

To Brian Ring for generously sharing your gifts and talents in the creative arts and graphic design fields. You are a blessing to me and everyone else who is privileged to work with you. I am continually amazed by your incredible designs.

To Jeff Krieger and Jacob Laureanti for creating my video with such short notice. You were an absolute joy to work with on this endeavor. I appreciate you and your team at Cinder Creative Video Production for wanting to share my story with the world.

To Craig Duswalt for allowing me to attend your Rockstar Book Camp. Thank you for teaching me to be an author and for encouraging me to write a book in 30 days. I will be forever grateful. You are a Rockstar in my book!

To Amanda Lemos for coming to my rescue with proofreading and formatting my manuscript. Thank you for being so generous with your skills and talents in these areas. You are a lifesaver!

To Ben Lawless for salvaging the data and photos from every computer and technical device that I have ever crashed. Thank you for sharing your knowledge and expertise to rescue me from yet another computer catastrophe.

To my Redemption Gateway church family for faithfully loving, praying for and supporting our growing brood. Thank you for encouraging us to stay the course in foster care and adoption. Thank you for the meals, babysitting offers and prayers. You kept us focused on God's perfect plan during our most difficult days.

To Matthew Braselton for your desire and willingness to discuss the tough issues in life. Your courage to tackle difficult situations head-on is inspiring. Thank you for your leadership and friendship, especially during the days when Rick and I were privately grieving the loss of our baby.

To Mark Andress for making work fun, but knowing when to be serious. Thank you for gathering the pastors to pray for us when we were hurting so deeply. Your leadership in Kids ministry and love for the Gateway families is a powerful combination.

To Luke Simmons for being my friend and pastor. Thank you for your commitment to teach with both truth and love. Thanks also for the 90 Day Tithe Challenge that forever changed our financial future. God has done great things through you, my friend.

To John Kronwald for your quiet, but influential presence. God has blessed you with a genuine desire and giftedness for relational ministry. Thank you for using those gifts to serve the Gateway congregation. I am honored to have the opportunity to work alongside you.

To Dale Thackrah for being a friend and counselor who shares both my joys and sorrows. Thank you for encouraging me with scripture as well as your own personal enthusiasm for whatever challenge I choose. Thank you for walking with and guiding others through some of their most difficult times as you continually point them to Jesus. The way you love and care for hurting people is inspiring.

To Josh Watt for your willingness to be used by God to impact the next generation. I am thankful to see how the Lord has grown you over the past few years and given you a desire to influence people of all generations through your teaching.

To Christine Reinke for providing your feedback regarding the content of this book. Some of your edits still make me laugh! You are a joy to work with at Gateway.

To Cristina Adams for tackling every task before you with quiet determination and a humble spirit. Thanks for sharing your wealth of talents with me in ministry.

To Tom Rowley for being the guy who has to plan for and recover from 1000+ guests each Sunday, not to mention all of our mid-week classes, events and meetings. Your humble, servant's heart blesses all of us who enjoy such a great experience in our facility each week.

To Austin Staheli for coming to my rescue when I have a tech issue and for "schooling" me on the best computers, phones and watches. Thanks for your infectious laugh and the way that you serve everyone on our staff team without question or hesitation.

To Angie and Dave Buchholz for loving and supporting our family in home school decisions, foster care drama and the endless web of information associated with adoption. Thank you for coming to our rescue with date nights and a much-needed getaway.

To Paul and Megan Swiatkowski for being so helpful with our tangible needs as well as the care of our seven children. You are brave souls!

To all the foster and adoptive families that we have been privileged to know in the past several years. Thank you for sharing your stories and for encouraging us to share ours. Together, we can make a difference!

To LaDonna Blakemore for all the ways you have loved me and my family. Thanks for sharing your story with me so I could better understand that my past does not define who I am in Christ.

To Diane Chan for quietly serving others in an endless number of ways. Thank you for encouraging our family through your kindness and generosity.

To Larry Ross for teaching me to "Philippians 4:8 the situation" through your teaching at Crosswork Singles Ministry, back in the day.

To Eric Worre for teaching me that we, as network marketing professionals, have a better way and that we also have a responsibility to go tell the world about it.

To Richard Bliss Brooke for giving me my first network marketing book in a Las Vegas coffee shop in the summer of 2012. Thanks for inspiring me on my first day of this incredible journey.

To Kimmy Merrill Brooke for being gracious and patient when a teary-eyed pregnant woman delayed your dinner plans in Vegas. Thanks for your kind offer to take our photo and commemorate my second encounter with Richard in December of 2013.

To John, Rosa, Luis, Janet, Danny, Clara, Nelly and Daniel for creating such a perfect evening and delicious meal before my final race. Spending time with family was the best way for me to finish strong.

To Paul Sr. and Jean Norman for spending time with me on such a special weekend at the end of my challenge. Conversations with you are always encouraging. I love and appreciate you both.

To Bobby Barrientos for making our stay in Boston for race #12 such a luxurious experience. Thank you for opening your home to us and for the post-race celebration and dinner.

To Peter Curtis for being my website guru. Thanks for making it easier for me to navigate the net and all that's involved.

To Paul Norman, Jr. (aka "Norm") for being the kind of friend who will fight to the bitter end for what he knows to be true. Thanks for selling me your Harley and for teaching me to keep it between the lines (and the mailbox). Thanks for your loyalty and care during some incredibly difficult times in my life. Everyone should have a friend and protector like you.

To Darby Mahon, Rebecca Marsh and Margaret Soberg of Christian Family Care Agency for supporting our family through the highs and lows of foster care and adoption. You are all deeply appreciated for your role in our family's journey.

To Crystal Thomson for being the best case worker we could ever hope for after becoming licensed. Thank you for advocating for children who most often have no voice in the decisions that impact their young lives.

To Graeme Wagner for all the ways that you have blessed me over the years. Thanks for the memories of our Mexico travels and the privilege of being a godmother to your sons. Your love and support is priceless.

To Rey Xuarez for teaching me that I deserve to live a healthier and more active lifestyle. Thank you for the countless hours you invested in my fitness journey so long ago.

To my Stretch Gang family in Georgia. Thank you for loving me for almost two decades of life. The ABC's, Tortilla Theory and Posture Checks will forever "haunt" me.

To Alex Bernal for the invitation to the Trail of Tribulation and for being used by God to open my eyes to what it means to be a follower of Christ.

To Marty Parris for the motorcycle rides that covered many miles and tons of Bible verses. Thank you for your patience with me as a new believer so many years ago. God used you to change my life and give me the courage to "go west". Snoopy Snap!

To Audra Berger and Shawna Thackrah for the high quality products and supplements that kept me going mile after mile.

To Lucy Activewear for helping me to find the perfect training wardrobe and race gear.

To Mountainside Fitness Gilbert for giving me a great place to train and a safe, fun environment for my children to enjoy.

To Dave McGillivray for planting the seed in 2010 for my goal of running the Boston Marathon. Thank you for challenging a room full of women with your key note speech to dream big and be victorious in our running endeavors.

I am forever grateful to these people and everyone else who inspired and supported my 12 in 12 Race Challenge. God blessed me through countless individuals and groups who may or may not have realized that they were a part of something that changed my life in endless ways. I thank God for each and every one of you and wish you a lifetime of dreams come true!

Special thanks to all the sponsors, organizers, event staff, volunteers and participants of the following races:

10/7/2012	San Jose, CA	P.F. Chang's Rock 'n' Roll Half Marathon
11/4/2012	Phoenix, AZ	Lady Speed Stick Women's Half Marathon
12/9/2012	Phoenix, AZ	Hot Chocolate 15K
12/16/2012	Fountain Hills, AZ	Athleta Iron Girl 5K
1/20/2013	Phoenix, AZ	P.F. Chang's Rock 'n' Roll Marathon
2/24/2013	San Diego, CA	Women's Half Marathon
3/2/2013	Phoenix, AZ	Phoenix Marathon
4/7/2013	San Francisco, CA	P.F. Chang's Rock 'n' Roll Half Marathon
5/27/2013	Syracuse, UT	Memorial Day Classic Half Marathon
6/2/2013	San Diego, CA	P.F. Chang's Rock 'n' Roll Marathon
7/13/2013	Holbrook, AZ	Bucket of Blood Half Marathon
8/18/2013	San Diego, CA	America's Finest City Half Marathon
9/29/2013	Providence, RI	P.F. Chang's Rock 'n' Roll Half Marathon

From the Author

My original plan for this book was to remind my children that they can set a goal and pursue it wholeheartedly in order to achieve their wildest dreams. As I began to write, I realized that it would also be my letter of gratitude to the countless individuals who took a journey with me that wasn't always easy, but definitely worth it. Because of feedback I have received from others, I now pray that my story will inspire and motivate you to dream big and chase after your own goals, as if money was no object and failure was not possible.

If you have lost your desire to dream, I want to encourage you with some valuable lessons. Most of these lessons were not new to me, but circumstances that unfolded in my life made them much more "real" after I set a goal to run twelve races in twelve consecutive months. I hope that you will be motivated by one, two or possibly all of these lessons in the pursuit of your own dreams.

I chose not to have this book professionally edited because I want it to also serve as my personal letter to you, the reader. I hope you can hear my voice in the words that I have put in writing for you. For whatever reason you have decided to read my story, I pray that you will be taken to a place where you will clearly see that all things are possible in Christ. Thank you for taking the time to read about my journey and see what can happen when faith trumps fear in the glorious pursuit of the seemingly impossible. Enjoy!

Two great reasons to run when you have seven children:
peace and quiet!

Contents

The Starting Line

In January 2010, I was taking a cycling class at a local gym. The room had a unique design that included one wall that was all glass. It gave me a nice view of the cardio area where others were walking, running, stair-stepping and sweating their way to better health. One guy, in particular, grabbed my attention when I realized that he had been running with great intensity for the same amount of time that I had been spinning. As I exited the room, I had a prompting to approach him and ask why he would ever spend that much time running like a hamster on a wheel. He informed me that he was training for a half marathon. My immediate response was, "I couldn't run that far if someone was chasing me with a gun."

Imagine, for a moment, that you were this guy. What would you do? How would you respond? Fortunately, for me, Anthony looked me straight in the eyes and said, "You're a runner. You just don't believe it yet." At that moment, I had no idea how true his assessment was. Upon hearing it, I simply began to list out all the excuses why I would never be able to run that far or that fast. Every one of my reasons started with "I can't" or "I don't" or "I could never". Anthony just stood there listening as I tried to convince him why I would never be able to achieve something like crossing the finish line of a race.

The irony in this conversation was that I wasn't a complete stranger to exercise. Almost two decades earlier, I had lost a lot of weight when a co-worker named Rey decided to teach me about healthy nutrition and exercise. He even gave me some mini training sessions on proper form for walking and running during our lunch breaks at work. It was because of his encouragement that I decided to transform my body and eventually become a personal trainer. When I grew weary of listening to my private clients whine about why they weren't successful with their goals, I decided to teach group fitness classes instead. I went on to complete several long-distance walking events and coach others on how to do the same. Later, I entered a physique transformation contest which led to some local celebrity and a feature article in Shape magazine.

With that background, it seemed odd that I would find myself quizzing a complete stranger in the gym about his training. However, life had taken over and I once again found myself overweight and unhappy with my fitness level and appearance. The worst part of it all was my negative outlook on the subject of fitness and a complete lack of confidence in my abilities. I had several accomplishments in the area of fitness, but somehow I had forgotten how strong I was in my "previous" life. It was the life I lived before I allowed other things to distract me from my own health and wellness. I never told Anthony that I had a background in personal training and fitness. I quickly found out that he was an employee in the gym where I met him. He was a personal trainer also. When I heard this, I just assumed that our conversation that day would be our last one unless I chose to hire him for training.

The next time I saw Anthony in the gym, he walked right up to me and said, "Let's get you running." A flood of emotions washed over me as I was led to a treadmill with no time to even protest the idea. He quickly gave me three simple tips and cranked up the treadmill so that I could put them into practice. He stood next to the machine for a short while to ensure that I was okay. After that, he disappeared into the gym while I continued on my first "real" run. When the treadmill finally stopped, I felt a sense of accomplishment that I hadn't known in quite a while. It felt good, but strange. From that day forward, whenever he saw me in the gym, Anthony would either give me a quick tip about running or see that I pushed myself a little farther in distance. When I would take his boot camp class, he made all of us go outside and run along the canal by the gym. Other people in the class started to complain as I walked into the room because they knew that we would all be running if I was there. Just a short time later, our gym closed without any forewarning. Anthony went to work for a different fitness center. I never had the opportunity to thank him once I ran my first race, Pat's Run in Tempe, Arizona on April 17, 2010. I was forty one years old and exceedingly proud that I ran the entire race, which was 4.2 miles. I'll never forget the feeling I had when I crossed the finish line to see my husband and children waiting for me. To top it off, we then ran the kids' "fun run" together as a family. It was .42 miles and finished inside Sun Devils Stadium on the 42 yard line in honor of Pat Tillman. While playing football at Arizona State, he wore the number 42 on his jersey.

It was a very symbolic day, in more ways than one. Seeing the excitement on my children's faces as they entered into the stadium was priceless. Just like me, neither of them had ever done anything like this before. My son was so thrilled to be running on the football field that he didn't even realize when he crossed the finish line. He kept running as fast as he could towards the end zone. We chased him through the crowds as we screamed for him to stop. Eventually, we caught up to him as he headed toward the stairs that led into the bleacher area. We took a moment to explain the purpose of a finish line and that he could stop running once he crossed it. It was hilarious to hear him express that he didn't really see any need in stopping since he was having so much fun beating all of us in the race. It was a fantastic adventure for our family and we still laugh about it.

Pat's Run was just the beginning of a journey that eventually led to other races. When my thoughts turned to running a longer distance, I researched various events in the Phoenix area. I found out that the Women's Half Marathon would be held in the fall of 2010 and I secretly wished that I had the courage to register for it. Since I couldn't really fathom the idea of running 13.1 miles, I put the idea aside and let my fear keep me from registering. I made jokes and used humor as a way to cover up the fact that I didn't want to risk taking a chance on failure. I could only envision a scenario that involved me not being able to accomplish the goal of a half marathon. I made a sarcastic comment in front of my friend Mandy that I didn't have the courage or the money to do that particular race. Soon after I said it, I was working in my office when I received an email confirmation from the Women's Half Marathon staff for my race registration. I was obviously confused because I knew that I hadn't registered for the event. I was still trying to figure out where the mistake was made when I received a text from Mandy, telling me that I then only needed the courage to make it happen. She had registered me for the race and it would be the first of many half marathons that I would run.

Because of the way that Anthony and Mandy looked past my excuses and fears, I eventually started to see the possibilities taking shape in my mind. Fortunately, Mandy and I have remained friends over the years and she has been a part of my life in many more ways than just running. As of the writing of this book, I still haven't seen Anthony or been able to thank him. It just hasn't seemed like the right time to let him know how much he impacted my life by giving me a renewed confidence in my abilities. My heart tells me that there is still more to do before I express my gratitude to the man who knew I was a runner long before I ever believed it myself. Anthony never mentioned the free training and advice that I received from him. He never made me feel guilty that he was giving away his time and wisdom for nothing, when he could have been helping a paying client. I still don't know why he chose to help me the way that he did. However, I do know that God used this stranger in the gym to change my life forever. Because Anthony freely shared his knowledge and experience to teach and encourage me, I started to believe that I was, in fact, a runner.

Our Family at Pat's Run
April 2010

Phoenix Women's Half Marathon
November 2010

Lesson #1:

Dare to Dream Again

When do we stop dreaming? Or worse, when do we stop pursuing our dreams? As children, we are taught that we can be anything we want in life. We are encouraged to dream big and go after our goals with no fear or hesitation. We learn that we can do whatever we set our minds to do with hard work and perseverance. We don't see boundaries or obstacles in our way. In our minds, we can do anything! As a Christian mom, I teach my children that they can do all things through Christ who strengthens them. (Philippians 4:13) Unfortunately, as years pass by, most of us stop dreaming and believing that we can actually succeed.

What causes us to lose our ability to dream with the same assurance and confidence that we had as children? Is it when other kids laugh at us or tease us on the playground? Is it when a teacher or mentor crushes our spirit by speaking negatively about us in front of our peers? Does it happen with divorce or the loss of a loved one? Perhaps we lose our ability to dream when we are neglected, abused or abandoned by a parent or guardian. There are many situations like these that can impact our desire to dream. It breaks my heart when I see people who desperately need to dream again, but they lack the belief that they can actually receive the desires of their heart.

I'm not quite sure when I stopped dreaming. Many of the situations that I mentioned previously came from my own personal experience. Over time, I must have decided that it was safer and easier to avoid the idea of dreaming altogether. Perhaps it wasn't one particular moment in time. Maybe it was a progression of circumstances that eventually wore me down and forced me to settle. Even though I can't put my finger on the exact day when my dreams were lost, I am absolutely certain of the day I started dreaming big again. It was June 7, 2012 at the national convention for a network marketing company that I had recently joined as a distributor. I received a last minute invitation from my friend, Barbara. She offered me a free ticket to the event if I could go on short notice. At first, I didn't think I would be able to work out all the details in order to travel to Las Vegas. My "can't mentality" took over before I could even sort through the specifics that would need to happen so I could attend the convention.

When I received the invitation, I was on vacation with my family in San Diego. I would have to drive home to Arizona, find childcare for my biological and foster children, take time off from work, pack a bag and then fly to Vegas in just a matter of days. It seemed impossible to get everything taken care of before the start of the conference. Fortunately, God handled the details and I was sitting on a plane on the way to my first ever direct sales convention. I had never been involved in any network marketing company, so I had no idea what to expect. Little did I know that my life was about to change dramatically. I can now look back and know with the utmost assurance that I was meant to attend that convention specifically. The Lord had a plan for my life that was about to take me on a journey that would radically alter the way that I viewed myself, my family, my ministry and so much more.

The founder and CEO of the company taught about the power of the "I Am" statement during the personal development session at convention that year. In a nutshell, he took us through a process of writing down things that we wanted to achieve in our lives as if they were already happening. I was baffled. I had never heard of anything so bizarre. I didn't understand the concept. I couldn't even think of a dream to write down. I started to feel the heat of embarrassment rise up my neck and into my face when I realized that I was unable to come up with even one thing to write. What had I gotten myself into? I thought I was going to an event for my business. I thought I was going to receive training about our product and the incredible business opportunity. What was all this talk about dreams, goal setting, vision boards and "I Am" statements? How could I escape this awkward situation? My pen was motionless and I was hoping that no one had noticed my blank stare at the empty lines on the page in front of me. I was frustrated and anxious. My mind was racing with thoughts of failure and embarrassment. I couldn't control the fear of looking stupid in a room full of "dreamers". I was as lost as last year's Easter egg!

Our leader continued to walk us through the process, asking questions and daring us to dream big. I looked around to see that others seemed to have no problem with this. I saw that Barbara's pen was moving non-stop. I was confused. My mind was more focused on how strange this concept seemed to me. As a Christian, I even felt awkward about writing the words "I Am" on a piece of paper unless I was referring to Jesus, who was the only "I Am" that I knew. Even so, I wanted to have a teachable heart and I knew that God had brought me to this convention for a reason. I just didn't know, at the time, what that reason was. So I did the only thing I could think of at that moment. I started praying. I asked God to help me because I was at a complete loss as to what I should do. I prayed that He would either give me wisdom on how to handle my uneasiness or give me words to write on the barren page in front of me. At that point, I would have been grateful to have an easy escape plan. Fortunately, He answered my prayer by giving me something to write.

As my pen began to move, I was shocked to see what I was writing. My mind was racing and my ideas started to flow onto the paper. While I continued to write down things that I wanted to achieve, the founder of the company reminded us all to remove any limiting thoughts or negativity from our minds. We were supposed to write as if money was no object and as if we could not fail in whatever goal we wrote. We were told to avoid any obstacles that might cloud our thinking or keep us from realizing our dreams. I continued to pray and the words filled my page. At the end of the session, I had written seventeen "I Am" statements. They ranged from things like financial and fitness goals to ways that I could change my community and ultimately impact the world. At the top of my list, I wrote, "Because of the great I AM and because of His grace…" as a header.

That statement alone helped me to focus more on the strength that I would gain from Christ above anything I could ever do on my own.

The items I wrote down that day immediately became my prayer list. I hung it next to my bed, on my bathroom mirror and in a variety of other places where I could easily access it for inspiration and accountability. It still brings me great peace and hope every time I read it for encouragement to continue pursuing my goals. When I see that God has already answered several of the prayers on my list, I know that I have no choice but to keep on going with my trust in the true I AM of my life. The list continues to grow as God puts more desires on my heart. Each time I sit down to write more statements, I feel stronger and more empowered. With time and practice, it has become easier for me to believe that I truly can do all things through Christ. Because of this on-going process, the Lord has introduced me to the idea of personal development. Although the term has different meanings for different people, I am able to see it as God's way of shaping me into the person that He designed me to be. It's just one of many ways that He has helped me to grow in my faith over the past several years. He is teaching me that I can choose faith over fear and win at anything I choose to do through His strength. What an incredible gift I have been given!

Out of all the initial statements I wrote back in 2012, one stood out to me more than the others. It read, "I am a marathon mom, soaring through twelve races in twelve months". Inside, I was laughing at myself. Imagine how ridiculous and impossible that must have felt for me to write something so audacious. At that moment in time, I had no belief whatsoever that I could someday realize that dream. It was too big, too involved and too far-fetched for someone like me to achieve. I had a list of excuses why I would never be able to accomplish this particular goal. I was a busy wife, mom, homeschooler, foster care advocate and business owner. I worked at my church. I had little to no time to focus on training. I felt out-of-shape and no way capable of running one marathon, let alone several. Regardless, I followed our CEO's instructions and sent myself a card with my "I Am" statements on it to use for motivation.

Since 2012, I have read all or part of that card every day as a reminder of how simple it can be to dream again and dream big. If you've never gone through an exercise like this, I highly recommend it. As a result of this one specific training, I have been changed in ways that I sometimes can't even put into words. I no longer use circumstances or people in my life as excuses not to dream again or chase after my goals. I can now visualize myself doing exactly what I have dreamed about and have been bold enough to share with others. I keep moving through open doors until God shuts one. Fortunately, He has continued to open those doors to opportunities that I could have never dreamed possible. I choose faith over fear and I am now teaching others to do the same. God used this particular network marketing company, its founder and its leaders to show me a way to grow in my faith, courage and belief. All of this has given me countless opportunities to then turn around and be a blessing to others. For that, I will be forever grateful.

Hanging out with Barbara Starley at one of the
many network marketing events we have
attended over the past several years.
November 2012

"A goal without a plan is just a wish."

-Antoine de Saint-Exupéry

Lesson #2:

Put Your Plans on Paper

Not long after I returned home from convention, I participated in a training call with various leaders and colleagues from my company. Our top distributor and #1 income earner was teaching about ways to be successful in business. The subject on this particular evening was about the importance of making plans, as well as booking events and meetings in advance. Jordan taught that once we have something in writing and on the calendar, we are more likely to follow through and do it. I had already seen the benefits of writing down my dreams during the "I Am" session at convention. At this point, I perceived the training call as simply the next step in the process of achieving my goals. He suggested that we pay in advance for events and any other expenses such as airline tickets, hotels and rental cars. I was intrigued by this simple tip that he assured us would make a big difference in our activity level and business success. As I listened to Jordan's advice and tried to apply it to my own business, I kept drifting over to the "I Am" statement that I had written about being a marathon mom. In my mind, I was able to easily apply the same concept of booking things in advance to my races. As soon as the call ended, I jumped online and booked six of the twelve races that I would need to complete in order to realize my dream of running them in twelve consecutive months.

This act alone set many things into motion for me. It meant that I was serious and ready to take on this "12 in 12 Race Challenge". I was committed. I started to tell others about it. At first, it was just my husband and closest friends who I knew would support me, no matter what. I wasn't quite ready for the questions like, "Are you crazy?" or "How can you afford that?" or "Do you really think you can run that many races?" Those questions eventually came, but they didn't derail me because I already had my plans in writing. They were scheduled and written on my calendar. I had paid for a lot of things in advance. I had already decided that I would take this challenge and see it through to the end. I had the support of those who believed in me and I knew that God had put this calling on my heart. It would only be a matter of time, twelve months to be exact, when I would have the confidence and experience to share with others the same instructions that had been given to me and hundreds of other entrepreneurs on that training call. Write it down. Schedule it. Commit.

Obviously, these tips can apply to many areas of our lives. I was listening to the call and saying to myself, "I've taught this before. How could I have forgotten it?" As a personal trainer many years prior, I would insist that my clients write all of their fitness goals down on paper. I would have them write down their measurements, weight, daily food consumption, exercise and other details in a journal. I also made them schedule their workouts on a calendar in advance. It kept them motivated and on track when the daily distractions of life started to creep in. By having things in writing, I could help them determine what changes needed to be made for them to be successful. While on the training call for my business, I realized that I was being reminded of the incredible value of writing down the things that I wanted to achieve.

In business, I keep a journal so that I can track my goals, remember my interactions with people and record success stories for inspiration. I've even followed the same principle with my prayer life. I write down my thoughts and prayers so that I can someday look back and see all the ways that the Lord has answered them. Seeing and sharing those answers to prayer keeps me focused on why I do what I do. It's my encouragement and motivation to keep going, especially when things get tough along the way. Taking the steps to commit to a plan and putting things on the calendar are the keys to success. Whether I am focusing on my fitness, my business or even my prayer life, I must ensure that I have it all in writing.

Lesson #3:

Give Grace to Others

Some "got it" and some didn't, and that's okay. Fortunately, my husband, Rick, understood how important this challenge was to me. He got it. He never questioned why. He never asked how we would afford it. He never used our busy schedule, family life or work commitments to make me feel guilty about training. On the contrary, he looked for ways to help motivate me. He made me go to the gym on days when I didn't want to be there. He would praise my training efforts, even when they were half-hearted. In his own patient and godly way, he led me through this process so that I could realize just how much we would both learn as we chose faith over fear to pursue the seemingly impossible things in life. He never wavered in his assurance that I would complete this challenge. He believed in me, even when I didn't believe in myself. His faith in what God was doing through this challenge was a blessing, especially during the times when I started to let fear creep into my plans.

As the date was drawing closer for my first race, I had a meeting with a friend named Betty, who wanted to discuss a volunteer program to support our church through Southwest Airlines. We met for lunch and discussed a variety of things such as church, volunteering, family and finances. When I began sharing my dream of running twelve races, she surprised me when she asked, "Do you need any airline tickets? If so, you can have two of my buddy passes to get to a race." I was floored! She didn't question my sanity. She didn't bring up any of the reasons that I could have used to avoid such a challenge. She didn't blink before she made an offer to be a part of my "crew" by helping me get to the first race. Betty got it and she wanted to be a part of the journey by offering a resource that she could freely give. I hadn't yet booked the flight for race number one. With Betty's offer, I realized that I could take a friend along with me or possibly even Rick. The idea of having my husband beside me still seemed like a long shot because, at the time, we had two of our own children and two foster children. Having someone watch them for a weekend might be a stretch. Nevertheless, I started to get excited about the possibility of kicking off my race challenge with someone there to cheer me across the finish line. In a very short time, all the details were in place. I would be running in San Jose with my amazing husband joining me for the adventure. We had two airline tickets, thanks to Betty. The rental car and hotel were booked and someone had agreed to watch our kiddos. This was really happening!

Just a few short weeks before race number one was to take place in San Jose, I was attending another one of our company's personal development and training seminars. My friends and teammates, Barbara and Cali, were with me. During one of the sessions, I received a text that made my heart sink as soon as I read it. The person who had agreed to watch our children while we were in San Jose let me know that they could no longer do it. Barbara looked over about the time my eyes started to fill with tears. When I told her about the text, she didn't even pause to take a breath before saying, "I'll do it." At first I wasn't sure that I had heard her correctly. She was a very busy woman and business owner with a packed calendar. I couldn't imagine how she would be able to clear her schedule to watch my children. However, she volunteered to do so without even glancing at her phone to see if she was free on those days. Barbara got it. She knew how much this challenge meant to me and how much I would be changed by the adventure that was about to unfold as a result of that one "I Am" statement. She was incredibly encouraging and eased my mind instantly. She has that gift, along with countless others. God had put her right there beside me for that exact moment and I was so thankful. Yet again, He had provided for my every need. This time, He did it by giving me this inspiring and supportive friend, who got it. Because of Barbara, I was able to run my first race of the challenge with the assurance that my children would be well cared for during my absence. As a result, race number one in San Jose was a great start to an unbelievable year of running.

For race number seven, I once again found myself in northern California. While in San Francisco, I was reunited with my dear friend, Laura. She was the first person I called when I decided to run the P.F. Chang's Rock 'n' Roll Half Marathon in the Golden Gate City. We had become friends in 2001 when I first moved to Arizona from Georgia. At that time, I had been praying that I would make a new friend because I was lonely and wanted someone to go to church with me on Sundays. God answered my prayer when I met this bubbly woman in a class at the gym. My first interaction with her came when I commented on her strong legs. Imagine what she must have been thinking when I, a complete stranger, told her that she had the prettiest calf muscles that I had ever seen. Fortunately, I didn't scare her off and we became great friends. Years later, she was living in a town north of San Francisco. She and her son, Logan, accompanied me from their home in Occidental to San Francisco for my race. We had a lovely carb-loading dinner in Little Italy before making our way to the hotel. Our conversations were light and easy, but filled with encouragement and inspiration. Laura and her sons have a way of making everyone around them feel special. They are crazy fun and make every encounter with them memorable. There was much laughter and silliness taking place during this race weekend and I felt truly loved that they would spend several days with me there. They selflessly went along to ensure that I had the best experience possible. Laura was at the starting line to take photos as I embarked on the first big hill of the day. She and Logan were patiently waiting at the finish line when I crossed it a couple of hours later with big tears in my eyes. I was overwhelmed with gratitude that my friend would want to support me in such a tangible way with her presence. She was a sweet reminder of just how much God loved me by blessing me with such encouraging friends. Needless to say, Laura got it.

Throughout the race challenge, there were countless other people who got it. They were the ones who offered their help, resources, tips, travel advice and countless prayers. They cared for our children, made signage to cheer me on the course and kept me focused on my ultimate goal. They messaged, texted, emailed and called me with a variety of inspiring quotes, songs and scripture references. They escorted me to starting lines and waited patiently for me to cross the finish line hours later. They tracked me along the race route, brought ice, dry socks, towels, peanut butter, oranges and ibuprofen. They constantly reassured me that I would be victorious in realizing my dream. I know that some were living vicariously through me on the journey. They needed me to succeed because they wanted proof that the seemingly impossible could be pursued and achieved. They showed me and my family the true meaning of love. It was blind, unconditional and never-ending. Sometimes I even felt like they may have wanted this more than I did. Those are the people who still inspire me today. They know my heart and they encourage me to go after whatever God is leading me to do. I know that I can count on them. I pray that they are assured that I will always be available to support them in the same way.

Obviously, not everyone in my life was overly supportive of my big adventure. Many of them just didn't understand the importance of it all to me. I heard many sarcastic comments and received plenty of questions about why I would ever choose to take on such a challenge. People wanted to know if spending the money on race registrations and travel was worth it. They questioned if my family resented the time I was away from them to train or participate in a race. Jokes were made about me paying to run on a public street for 26.2 miles when I could do it for free on any other day of the week. Some would ask if I actually completed the race on foot or if I had to be carried across the finish line. I knew that most of the comments were harmless and just for fun. However, I also realized that a few people did not actually want me to succeed. By completing this challenge, I would be revealing that excuses were no longer acceptable to me. If God allowed me to realize a victory in this, it would validate my belief that I truly could do all things through Him. Through His strength, I would prove that a busy wife, mom and business owner, who homeschooled her kiddos, advocated for foster children and enjoyed a great job in ministry, could actually accomplish something so outrageous. I, nor those closest to me, would ever be able to use people or circumstances again as excuses not to try. Instead, we would have to use those same people and circumstances as the reasons why we must chase after our goals.

From my own past, I knew all too well how paralyzing it was when I allowed fear and excuses to control my thoughts. As soon as a big idea or dream would enter my mind, I would counter it with thoughts like, "I'm too busy", "I'm too fat" or "I'm too old". By taking me through this difficult but rewarding challenge, God was teaching me how to take my limiting beliefs and negative thoughts captive. The "stinking thinking" had held me back far too long. Throughout the challenge, I worked hard to counter my excuses with the reasons why I must follow through to my goals. I realized that the easy way out would have been to quit. I would have been able to choose from a variety of things that prevented me from finishing the race challenge. However, my choice to give up would have given some people the ammunition to point out that I had taken on too much and that I shouldn't have even started such a tough and time-consuming journey. I certainly didn't want to be one more excuse that others could use to avoid stepping out in faith on their own challenges. Because of this, I prayed that God would help me see that any setback along the way was simply a setup for a comeback. I also prayed that He would give me the peace and humility to view other's negative opinions of my challenge with grace. Initially, I must admit that I was hurt by the reactions and comments of a few critics in my life. However, over time I was able to see that God was using my races and my story to inspire and motivate others. Some of those same people who first thought I was crazy for doing this now have written down their own goals and have started their own challenges. That makes it all worthwhile.

Looking back now I can see clearly who got it and who didn't. I truly love them and I pray for them all to find the strength and courage to chase after their own goals. I know that there may come a day when those who didn't initially get it will realize that they too want to dream again. I understand first-hand the desperation and frustration that can come when someone feels weak, hopeless or lost.

I have experienced the anxiety that results from thinking that I have to settle because I can't achieve the things that I secretly wish I could do. When I encounter people who have obviously gone through many of my same struggles, I try to reach out and encourage them in any way possible. I then wait for them to take the first step towards their goals so that I can join them for the rest of their journey. Ultimately, my desire is to be at their "finish line" to celebrate with them and see the incredible joy that comes when they experience any sort of victory in their lives.

I see this same dynamic also play out in my ministry. I share my faith on a regular basis with people. Sometimes they get it and sometimes they don't. The rejection I receive is often difficult to handle, especially when it comes from people that I love and cherish dearly. I want desperately for them to know the freedom that can only be found in Christ. However, I've learned over the years that it's not my job to convince them. God is the only one who can do that. I can't change their hearts or their minds. That is not my job, nor is it my responsibility. I am simply called to share my story. I can only share what God has done for me and pray that someday He will soften their hearts to know and appreciate what He did through Jesus' death on the cross.

Besides, for a very long time, I was someone who didn't get it. Even though I professed to be a Christian, I didn't actually come to know the Lord personally until October 31, 2000. I had been invited by one of my few Christian friends to a church event that was supposed to be an outreach on Halloween. It was called the Trail of Tribulation. Sounds scary, huh? Actually, it turned out to be the event that God would use to open my eyes to His power, strength and grace. Even though people had been sharing the gospel with me for most of my life, it wasn't until that particular moment in time that I became a Christian. I was thirty-one years old and my life was never the same again. There aren't words to express my gratitude to everyone involved in that event, especially my friend Alex, who invited me to attend. The Lord used Alex to share his story with me and I was ultimately changed forever. Because of God's work in my life, through a faithful and patient friend, I finally got it.

In my business, I have had plenty of opportunities to help people understand the possibility of financial and time freedom. I have seen and heard many great success stories in the network marketing profession. I personally know people who have made fantastic incomes in our industry and then have gone on to help others do the same. Many times, when I share the opportunity involved with my company, people get it right away and they are ready to build their business and see their entrepreneurial dreams come true. Other times, I get the crossed arms, squinty eyes and furrowed brows as they question whether or not I am nuts to be a part of the network marketing profession. One of the most disheartening situations for me is when I see enthusiastic business builders get discouraged and quit after they encounter a person who doesn't get it. I have dealt with this same discouragement while meeting with someone that I am sure would understand the business opportunity, but then I realize that they don't. I have gone into a meeting thinking that the light will go on quickly and then it doesn't. I have to fight the feeling to give up and stop sharing with people. To regain my focus and perspective, I grab my journal, read through the pages and remember that it's not my job to convince anyone of anything. I am simply called to share the blessings in my life. It's okay that others don't yet get it. Lord willing, in time, they will.

I am a perfect example of someone who took their dear sweet time to join the best business model ever created. It was only after five years of looking at the product and opportunity of my company that I made the choice to be a part of it. I'm truly thankful that my friend, Barbara, didn't give up on me during that time. Without her diligence, I could have missed out on the opportunities that I have enjoyed since becoming a member of this profession. I would have missed out on that first convention. My "I Am" statements wouldn't have been written. The race challenge would have never happened. As a result, you wouldn't be reading this book. For all of these wonderful things, I thank God for Barbara. She loved me just the same, even when I didn't quite yet get it. She answered countless questions for me over a long period of time. She met with me on several occasions and explained much of the opportunity over and over again until I fully understood the business model. She was consistent in her desire to share with me and she helped me to see the possibilities that were in my future. She never seemed to grow weary of returning my calls and encouraging me through the process, even when there was no guarantee that I would ever fully get it. In my eyes, that's the way we should always be with those who don't understand what we are trying to share with them: understanding, patient and full of grace.

Laura Marra, Logan, Me and Branden
Occidental, CA before Race #1

Race #1 – Done!
San Jose, CA
October 2012

Me and Laura at the starting line
Race #7 – P.F. Chang's
Rock 'n' Roll Half Marathon

A little finish line fun
San Francisco, CA
April 2013

Lesson #4:

Remember That Lessons are Caught, Not Taught

Race number two was the Lady Speed Stick Women's Half Marathon in Phoenix on November 4, 2012. It was a fairly uneventful race, but it was one of the best managed events that I had ever experienced. The race staff, sponsors and volunteers were super encouraging. The course was well planned and there was a good security presence for the entire 13.1 miles. I had run this race previously, so I basically knew what to expect from the course. What I had not expected was what happened after I crossed the finish line to meet my family. At this event, they usually have a member of a local ROTC group put the medal over your head right after you cross the finish line. It's a pretty cool moment that feels extra special because someone in uniform is congratulating you and presenting you with a medal for completing the race.

On this day, I left the finisher's area after receiving my medal and quickly found my family. Before I could say a word, one of my foster sons yelled, "Mommy! You came back!" At first, I thought it was a funny thing for him to say. Then I realized that he might have actually thought that I was leaving and not coming back to my family. Because he and his brother had recently been removed from another foster home and brought to us, I knew that his level of security with our family might not be very high at that moment. I sensed that I had done a poor job of explaining a race like this in terms that a four-year-old in his situation could comprehend.

At that moment, I knew that God was giving me a teaching opportunity for all of my children, both biological and foster. I sat down with them and started to explain that there are people who won't walk away or quit when things get tough. I let them know that even though some people may give up on themselves or others in difficult times, that would not be the case with me or their father. I tried to use my running and race training as an example that they might understand. I explained that even when things get tough for me in a race or in life, I would always come back to them. I wanted them to feel safe and secure in the fact that they would not be left alone or abandoned. They would never have to worry about mommy or daddy leaving them or giving up on them. I wasn't quite sure how much they understood, but they all seemed to be reassured after my explanation at the finish line.

It was then that I decided to seize every opportunity after a race to teach them about hard work, perseverance, determination and responsibility. More importantly, I wanted them to experience what I had been telling them about faith and living in the strength that can only come from God. My prayer was that they would see my successes in the challenge as gifts from my heavenly father. I wanted them to experience the feeling of accomplishment when I crossed the finish line, especially since they had seen me go out for training runs and come back exhausted. They watched me work hard and push myself to my physical limitations. They saw me eat grilled chicken and broccoli when I really wanted ice cream for dinner. They had access to me "behind the scenes" and now I wanted them to see the result of all that work. I tried to help them understand that ultimately the medal was not what I was running for in this challenge. It was just a symbol and souvenir of the race. It meant nothing more and nothing less.

My primary goal for all of these races was to experience the different things that I would learn from them along the way. I wanted my children to know that they could truly do whatever God put on their heart, if they would simply trust and obey Him on the journey. I had said this to them many times and gave them several scriptural references to encourage them biblically. It was time that I showed them these principles in action. I knew that my words had power to influence my children, but I believed that my actions would speak much louder than words when I was encouraging them to dream big, set goals, overcome challenges and chase after the true victories in life.

This lesson played out in real life during race number three. At the expo for race number two, my eight-year-old daughter was drawn into a booth where they had beautiful participant shirts that were purple with butterflies on them. The color of the shirts alone was enough to make her want to run her own race. The butterflies were just an added incentive. Once she learned that she would receive that shirt if we registered as a mother/daughter team for the upcoming Iron Girl race, she was practically begging me to do it. Knowing my daughter as I do, this was pretty surprising. She's a swimmer, not a runner. Even though I had already scheduled a race for that month, I decided that it was important for us to do the Iron Girl together. That said, we registered there on the spot and headed home with our cool new running shirts. This race in Fountain Hills, Arizona was only a 5K, which was much shorter than my normal races. However, this event meant more to me than anything. It was the one that I would experience with my daughter.

On race day, I woke up sick. It was one of those "all over" kind of bugs. I had a headache, sore throat, upset stomach and body aches. My husband quickly reassured me that I didn't have to do this race. I had already done another race that month, so this would not take away from my total number of 12 events. He didn't want me to take any chances on getting sicker or not being able to finish the run. I definitely entertained the idea of staying in bed and letting him take care of me. However, as soon as the bedroom door swung open and my daughter came marching in with her cool purple shirt, I rolled out of bed and got dressed. Besides, she had recently dealt with her own health issues when she had an allergic reaction after being around a cat. It was a very scary episode that had happened several days before and her eyes were still somewhat swollen and red. If she wasn't going to let that stop her, then I would just have to get over myself and join her for the run. We couldn't miss this chance to do something so fabulous together.

Nothing about this race was "normal" for me. I didn't even wear my regular running gear. I put on some sweatpants and a long sleeved shirt to help with the chills that I was experiencing. I looked and felt like I had been hit by a truck. Graesen never noticed. She was too excited to have the chance to run with her mom in matching shirts. We arrived at the starting line and I had to fight against the urge to let her know how sick I was. I was beginning to accept the fact that I would most likely not be able to run. It was then that I noticed how excited she was to be amongst all the people, hear the music, see the medal that she would receive later and know that she was going to do it all with me. Any notion that I had about bailing on this race went out the window right away. If it was at all within my power, I knew that I was going to finish this event.

Soon after we started and the initial excitement calmed down, Graesen asked if we could walk for a while. I was more than happy to oblige that request. She then asked me to carry her jacket which she had refused to leave with her father at the starting line. This was going to be interesting. About a mile into the race, I noticed a conversation that was taking place behind us. Before I could make out the words that were being spoken, I could hear the tone and I knew that it was not a fun, casual discussion. As the people got closer to us, I realized that it was obviously a mother and daughter who were approaching. The mother was verbally berating her daughter because she wanted her to run. She was saying, "I cannot believe that you can't run this short distance. You are still a kid. You should be ashamed of yourself. You are just lazy. You should have more stamina than this. I'm going to hire a calisthenics coach to get you into shape." Instantly, my heart sank. The negativity in her words crushed me. If I could have run away at that moment, I would have. It was painful to hear such harshness from a mother to her daughter.

I glanced over at Graesen and saw that she was obviously affected by what she was hearing. I gave her my best reassuring smile in hopes that she understood that we would talk about the situation later. As the woman and her daughter passed us on the route, I was able to see that the girl was probably no more than ten or twelve years old. I immediately felt sorry for her. I started to imagine what her teenage years would hold for her if she faced this much criticism and shame over a simple 5K run. Graesen and I spent most of the remainder of the race talking about this situation and what we could learn from it.

Eventually, our discussion returned to the race and then shifted to the fact that Graesen was now ready for it to be over. The excitement connected to the cool race shirt was gone. She was hot and uncomfortable. Remember, this is only a 5K. However, it must have seemed like an eternity to her since she had never done anything like this before. I tried to give her an idea of how great she would feel once she accomplished her goal of finishing the race. I expressed how much she would enjoy the moment when the medal was placed around her neck, symbolizing her victory. She would achieve her dream that began with the pretty purple shirt at the runner's expo. None of this seemed to matter to her now. She was tired, hungry and ready for it to end. At that moment, God gave me some help. We made a turn onto a street that was the final stretch of the race. We were now running straight for the huge fountain that is the centerpiece of the city of Fountain Hills.

When built, it was the world's tallest fountain and held that record for over a decade. On this day, as the world's fourth tallest fountain, it was still a beautiful sight to behold. Approximately every fifteen minutes, it sprayed water as high as 560 feet. As soon as it came into view, I looked over at Graesen and told her that we should focus on it as we sprinted to the finish line. This tip of re-directing focus was one of the original three tips that Anthony gave me back in 2010. I was so thankful that God reminded me of such a simple way to get through a temporarily uncomfortable situation. Graesen didn't seem all that excited about running so fast, until a man on the sidewalk encouraged her by saying, "Good job, Graesen. Grab your mom's hand and help her get to the finish line!" Now this guy was a stranger to us. He knew nothing about my race challenge, me or my daughter. God, in all his sovereignty, had placed him in the perfect location with the perfect words to help me keep her moving. The only way he knew Graesen's name was because it was listed in bold letters on her racing bib. However, by using it in such a personal way, he was able to motivate her when I couldn't. By giving her the instruction to help me finish, he also gave her the permission and desire to run faster than I had ever seen before. This was no longer my race challenge. It was hers.

Try to imagine the scene. My eight-year-old and I were now running down a slight hill towards this awesome spray of water on a bright, beautiful December morning. She was experiencing the joy and feeling of victory that I had been trying to explain to her after each of my races. Her face was beaming. To top it all off, she was once again recognized by name. As we turned into the finisher's chute, this is what we heard: "Ladies and gentlemen. Help me welcome young Graesen Marrs and her mom from Gilbert, Arizona to the finish line. Great job, Graesen! You did it!" Graesen looked over at me with a face that I had never seen before. She said, "Mom, did you hear that? He said my name!" My response was, "I certainly did, Graesen. It's because you are a winner."

Just before we crossed the finish line, she leaned over to give me a high five. That moment in time will forever be engrained in my memory. It was the highlight of my race challenge. My daughter now knew the significance of achieving a goal and realizing a dream. She understood that she was also a winner. She was a finisher, not a quitter. She was victorious. As we got our medals, I couldn't help but stare at her. I couldn't imagine what she was thinking. When I was a young girl, I never experienced something like this. I could only hope and pray that she would carry this achievement in her heart as a reminder of what can happen if she trusts God, works hard and perseveres as she chases after her goals. Once we received our medals and finisher's breakfast box, it was time for a few photos.

I was feeling worse than I had been before the race, but on the outside, I was beaming. I wanted this moment and these feelings to last forever between Graesen and myself. The moment passed a little too quickly when Graesen asked, "Mom, can we go home now?" I was shocked that she would want to leave before walking around the finish line area and enjoying all that there was to do. I assumed that she would want to show off her medal and talk about the highlights of her first official running event. On the contrary, she informed me that she just wanted to go home and play with her brothers. And just like that, we were done. She hopped into the van, took off her medal, laid it on the seat beside her and started enjoying her breakfast. I watched her in the rearview mirror for the entire trip home. My husband and I discussed what she might remember about this race when she grew up. Tears welled up as I realized that I couldn't recall any victorious moments like this with my biological mother. She had passed away when I was very young and my memories with her were now few and faded. I could only hope and pray that if something were to happen to me, Graesen would always remember the day that she ran a race with her mom and the lessons that we both learned along the way.

Later that day, I revisited the situation that took place with the mother and daughter that had passed us on the race course. I asked Graesen to let me know if I ever made her feel like she wasn't good enough or if I did anything to make her feel ashamed or insufficient. I'm sure that I've messed up plenty of times in this area, but I wanted her to know that I would never intentionally insult or belittle her. Because of what happened during the race that morning, I knew that God was giving me another teaching opportunity that I would not soon forget. I can still see the woman and her daughter in my mind. I can hear the words that were spoken so harshly and I can feel the sympathy that I had for the young girl as I listened to her try to reason with her mother. My prayer is that I will always be a source of encouragement and a godly example for my daughter, as well as all of my children. I'm not perfect, by any means, but I want them to see and feel unconditional love and support from me. I know that the best way I can accomplish this is to build them up with my words and show them with my actions how much I cherish them and believe in their abilities.

This all goes back to how we can lead by example, not just words. Most often, people are watching what we do more than they are listening to our words. I see this play out in so many areas of my life, but especially at home. I can't just tell my children to dream big and chase after their goals. I shouldn't just tell them that they need to love others, even when they might be dealing with people who aren't being very lovable. I can't just tell them that I love them with words. I must show them with my actions. Words will only carry us so far. What matters is how we live out the lessons that we teach our children. They are watching. They are catching what they see more than hearing what we say.

In ministry, I have seen this lesson at work as well. People I meet with are watching what I do more than they are listening to what I actually say. I can counsel someone all day long about a particular area of life that they should focus on changing. I can quote scripture and explain why God would bless them for their obedience and trust in Him. I can go as far as talking about how I would do things if I were them. However, what seems to impact people most is when they see these principles played out in my own life. I can teach them the principle of stewardship behind The 90 Day Tithe Challenge, but they don't seem as interested until I share our family's story in the area of finances. When I describe the actual steps that we took in ninety days to pay off debt and prepare ourselves for financial freedom, I paint a picture that includes the difficulties, as well as the rewards, for participating in such a life-changing endeavor. That's when the "light bulb" moments seem to happen. They realize that I am not just telling them what they should do. I am showing them that my faith in God's sovereignty grew as I trusted Him through a time of painful financial challenges.

In my business, I sometimes struggle with the fact that people pay for and attend a training event without ever implementing any of the lessons taught that day. All the notes were taken and people nodded when they were asked if they understood. At the end of the training, they were excited to go home and get things done. However, without a compelling story or example for them to follow, most people will never even re-visit their notes or remember exactly the reason they ever went in the first place. They need an example to follow, not just bullet points on a page. I must confess that I have failed as a leader to do this at times. I'm continually growing and trying to learn how I can set a better example for others. When I encourage my team to attend events and invest in their businesses, I know that I must also do the same. I've seen the difference in participation vary greatly when I am practicing what I preach in this area. My team wants to see that I am willing to do more than talk about success. They want to see that I am also doing the work myself. I've seen it happen over and over again in every area of my life. Lessons are caught, not taught.

I pray that my sweet Graesen remembers this day forever.
Race #3 - Athleta Iron Girl 5K in Fountain Hills, AZ
December 2012

"Challenges are what make life interesting. Overcoming them is what makes life meaningful."

- Joshua J. Marine

Lesson #5:

View Challenges as Opportunities

I have always loved the word "challenge". If someone were to add that word to just about anything, I would be all in for whatever it was. I've participated in a physique transformation challenge, The 90 Day Tithe Challenge, The Biggest Loser at Home Weight Loss Challenge, The 30 Day Gratitude Challenge and now the 12 in 12 Race Challenge. Something about a challenge gets me going. I respond well to that word. During my race challenge, I started to clearly see that the "obstacles in the road" were always great opportunities for me to grow as a person. God would use them to increase my self-control, stewardship, patience, perseverance, commitment and determination. He would also use them to humble me and teach me some principles that I would be able to implement in my own life before going on to teach others the same. Many times, these challenges are inconvenient and sometimes very painful. I have had to examine my own heart, selfishness, need for control and lack of faith along the way.

Race number six was the Phoenix Marathon on March 2, 2013. This event was crazy! I had previously run it in 2012 which was the inaugural year when they only had the half marathon option. At that time, it was probably my favorite running event to date. They had the best finish line area of any other race that I had completed. The staff was incredibly friendly. Runners and volunteers alike seemed to be having a blast. However, in 2013, they included both the half and full marathon options. I decided to do the full marathon to see what it would be like to complete it. Since it was a qualifier for the Boston Marathon, I secretly wanted to see if it would be a good opportunity for me to focus on that goal as well. However, this race turned out to be a series of events that nearly made me want to re-consider my decision to run at all.

ELLEN MARRS

At 4:00am on race day, I found myself sitting in dead still traffic on the interstate off ramp in Mesa. We had been forewarned that if we weren't in the parking lot by a certain time, we would miss the bus that would transport us to the starting line. Since the road located closest to the start of the race would be closed early in the morning, we had no other options to get there except the shuttle. For that reason alone, I left my home extra early. Rick had to work and was unable to go with me. So there I was, sitting in my car on the freeway and wondering if I would ever get close to the parking lot where I was supposed to catch the bus. After approximately 45 minutes, I called Rick in tears. I was ready to quit and head home if the traffic ever started moving again. The anxiety of waiting in bumper-to-bumper traffic had me frazzled. My head hurt. My stomach was churning. I had to go to the bathroom. That was a deadly combination for someone who was about to run 26.2 miles. Rick reminded me of my goals, encouraged me to pray for the situation and assured me that I would make it to the starting line on time. I continued to express my frustration to him, but ultimately decided to trust his instincts and pray that God would make it possible for me to run the race that day. Within minutes of our conversation, a barrage of motorcycle officers flew past me and headed toward the front of the never-ending line that I was sitting in on the ramp. Shortly thereafter, the traffic started to move and we were on our way. Thank God for the Mesa Police Department! They saved the day. I parked my van, grabbed my gear and joined the crowds of people who were sprinting to get on the last bus that was going to the starting line.

Once we arrived at the staging area, I tried to salvage my normal "race morning routine" by scarfing down my banana and last sips of water while waiting in line for the porta potty. After several races, I had developed a consistent routine that seemed to work for me to have energy and peace of mind at the beginning of a race. Unfortunately, that schedule would not go according to my plans for this event. While I was in the porta potty, which was quite a distance from the starting line, I heard the gun go off to signal the start of the race. Immediately, I heard a rumbling along "outhouse row" as

32

countless runners were trying to finish their business, get their gear in order and head out for the race. My headache returned and my stomach began to churn again. How could this be happening? Didn't they know that the traffic was ridiculous? Couldn't they delay the race long enough for us to go to the bathroom? I was still trying to peel off my sweatshirt, pin on my race bib and fasten my running belt as I ran down the hill to the starting line. As my feet hit the pavement of the road, I looked down the hill to see that the majority of the runners were long gone. It was quiet and lonely as I started this race basically on my own. There was no time to warm up, socialize, enjoy the pre-race entertainment or even call Rick to let him know that I had made it to the starting line. This race was already challenging every basic instinct that I had to be in control, organized and prepared. I hadn't even run the first mile yet! Fortunately, once I got started, I was able to settle down and enjoy the beauty of the desert landscape around me. I was running through the mountains in Usery Park, which was mostly downhill at this point. As I enjoyed the easy terrain, I turned my thoughts to praying that God would bless me with a smooth run after such a chaotic morning. Little did I know that He had other plans to stretch and grow me on that day.

The first half of the race was mostly uneventful. We ran through some really nice neighborhoods and experienced the support of people who were along the route, cheering for us. It felt good to see friendly faces and enjoy some of Arizona's finest weather conditions. I had started to feel a slight burning sensation in the arch of my right foot, but tried to ignore it in hopes that it would go away. I assumed that I was developing a blister or two on my foot. Since I had never had a blister during my training or any of my races, this came as a surprise. Unfortunately, it only worsened and then started to spread to other parts of my foot. Later I found out that it was most likely caused by the nice downhill slope that I had enjoyed during the first part of the race. My foot was slipping in my shoe a bit more than usual because of the decline of the course elevation. That can cause blisters. At the halfway point of the race, I decided to stop and check out whatever was actually causing the pain I was feeling. When I took off my shoe, I wanted to cry. I not only had a blister in the arch of my foot, but I also had a large fluid-filled bubble that spanned across the top part of the underside of my foot. To make matters worse, I had a few more on the bottom of a couple of my toes. Because of my experience with helping others deal with blisters in long-distance walking events, I knew that I needed to pop, drain and bandage the affected areas if I was going to be able to finish this race. I still had another 13 miles to go at this point. When I approached the medical crew, I was met with a girl who appeared to be no more than fourteen or fifteen years old. She argued that I shouldn't pop the blisters and proceeded to wrap gauze and tape around my foot, on top of the blisters.

Just a few minutes later, I was back on the course when I realized that this was not going to be a good fix. I had so much crap wrapped around the middle of my foot, it felt like I had a mini speed bump in my shoe. Every time my foot hit the ground, it rolled forward in such a way that it made my toes cram into the end of my shoe. After a few more miles, I stopped again to un-wrap this massive ball of bandages to find that I now had blisters on the tops of each of my toes because of the way my foot had been wrapped. It was turning into a nightmare. Everything in my soul was screaming, "Just quit already! This is nuts!" As I sat down to figure out what to do, I started to pray. I wanted God to make it very clear if I was supposed to throw in the towel at this point. Instead of doing that, He gave me an idea. I took one of the pins provided to secure my race bib off of my shirt and used it to pop all of the blisters on my right foot. I even took off my other shoe and popped the ones that were starting on my left foot. I dried off my feet, put on my socks and once again returned to the race route. The burning sensation in my shoes was a constant reminder that this was not going to be an easy race to finish. I had to find the opportunity in this situation and move forward quickly before I had time to consider making that call for someone to come and get me.

As only He can do, the Lord took my mind off of my feet pretty soon after I got back on the course. As I approached a rather large intersection, a police officer came over and started apologizing to a small crowd of runners that was just in front of me. He explained that he was going to have to stop us at the intersection so that traffic could be allowed to move. This was a huge shock to many of us because this race was a qualifier for the Boston Marathon. The seconds or minutes that are spent waiting for traffic to cross could cost someone their qualifying time. By now, I had already determined that my feet were not going to allow me to go as fast as I had hoped. But for others, they were really upset that they might lose their opportunity to run the Boston Marathon. At first there were some minor protests from the runners, but then we all started to realize that a serious situation was developing at the intersections.

Because of the layout of the half and full marathon courses, the roads had been closed for hours that morning and people had been stuck in their cars for long periods of time. I looked up to see a guy getting out of his truck and screaming at the runners as well as the police officers. Several people were cursing at us from their cars and others were giving us the "one finger wave" to show their frustration over having to wait for the runners to pass by before they could go on their way. Up until this point, I never used a headset or radio during a race because I gained inspiration from the sounds and conversations that could be heard along the route. However, as soon as I realized that we were being threatened by the crowds of people who were stuck in traffic, I immediately put on my earphones and cranked the tunes up to drown out some of the harsh language and threats. I was scared, but so thankful for the police officers who were posted along the course. They did a great job of watching out for us, as well as trying to help the people who were caught in traffic.

I had only run about a mile or so farther when I was stopped for another intersection crossing. I had a few minutes to thank the officers for being there. I also seized the opportunity to express my gratitude for the manner in which they were handling all of the insults and hand gestures that were being sent their way. They were bearing the brunt of the frustration from people who were caught in the race traffic. The officers certainly didn't deserve to be treated this way.

They were very gracious and eventually waved me through the crossing. Minutes later, I could hear a muffled sound coming from behind me. As I turned around to see what was happening, I found myself staring at the front end of a car that was headed straight for me. The sound I had heard was the officers screaming for me to get out of the way. Before I had a chance to even think about what I was going to do, I held up my hand as a signal for the driver to stop and then started waving my other arm to get him to pull out of the runner's lane. He had obviously gotten disoriented with all of the traffic and runners on the street. He ended up turning into our lane in an attempt to get out of the area as quickly as possible. I started screaming as loudly as I could and continued to motion for him to leave the lane. There was a small crowd of runners just a few hundred yards ahead of me, so I felt the need to do something before a lot of people got hurt. As he approached me, I realized that I needed a different plan. Just as I started to move toward the sidewalk, he made a sharp turn between the cones within about 15 feet of me. From there, he was able to move into a regular traffic lane. By this time, one of the officers had jumped onto his motorcycle and was riding alongside the car and banging on the guy's window. I stood frozen for what seemed like forever when the officer came back to check on me and ask if I was okay. I can't remember what I said to him at that point, but he joked that they had an open position with their traffic division if I was ever interested. I tried to laugh and not give in to the urge to cry as I thanked him once again and started back on my way.

At this point, I stopped asking myself, "What more could possibly happen today?" I was growing weary and losing sight of why I was even doing the race. I called Rick and gave him a long list of things to bring to the finish line. I would need some medical supplies for my feet, ice packs to reduce the swelling, ibuprofen for my pain and a big jar of peanut butter because I wanted to drown my sorrows in my favorite comfort food. He tried to encourage me as best he could on the phone, but it just wasn't enough to help me regain my desire to keep going. The challenges were beginning to outweigh any opportunity that I could see in such a crazy situation. Once again, I asked the Lord to make the rest of my run easier and more enjoyable. That's when He decided to make me laugh, at least for a minute or two.

As I was doing my best to actually run on my "swiss cheese" feet, I approached a woman who was walking on the route. She had one hand on her left hip and was swinging her right arm as if she was using it to propel herself forward. Her head was tilted and she was looking down. I thought she was singing, but then realized as I got closer that she was actually talking to herself. I asked her if she was okay and she replied, "Yes. I'm just Tinkerbell." When I tried to determine if she actually did say those exact words, she repeated the same statement. After I quizzed her a little longer, I realized that she was in need of medical attention. Her eyes were glazed over and the things she was saying to me didn't make any sense. Then she started to cry as she explained that she wasn't used to our heat in Arizona and that her friends had left her behind when they decided to run ahead in their attempts to qualify for Boston.

Just a few minutes later, she appeared as if she was going to lie down or fall. I begged her to stay on her feet because I would never be able to pick her up or carry her to a medical tent. I started asking her random questions to keep her engaged in conversation until I could get someone to help. Now try to imagine this scene for a moment. I was hobbling along as best I could on two blister-covered feet. I was tired and emotionally drained from all that was happening. I encountered this woman who was very close to passing out and I didn't have a clue what to do with her if she fell. As I was trying to assess the situation and determine if it would be safe to just run ahead for help, I heard a voice coming from the sidewalk. It was an older lady who was walking next to our race route, pulling a rolling suitcase behind her. She made me think of a gypsy or possibly someone who was still living in the 1960s, circa the Woodstock era. She had on a long, flowing skirt with some ancient-looking Birkenstocks sandals on her feet. She was talking to us, but it took a minute for me to determine what she was saying exactly. She repeated herself, "Do either of you ladies want some of my magic tonic water?

It's only two dollars." WHAT? Are you kidding me? This can't really be happening. I must be on some crazy reality show where I am being "punked". I honestly thought for a few brief moments that my friends had decided to have fun with me and this race challenge. My guess was that they had hired some really great actors to drive me crazy for 26.2 miles. There is no way that someone is actually trying to sell us "magic tonic water" from a rolling suitcase during the Phoenix Marathon. When I tried to explain that I needed to get help for my fellow runner, the woman from the sidewalk assured me that her water would take care of any ailments that we might have. She repeated the price again, as if we would seriously consider it. Finally, my frustration started to feel more like anger. I was clueless about how I was going to handle all of this chaos and craziness. I held up my hands, told the woman that we were trying to finish a marathon and then showed her that I had no place on me to carry the money that she was asking from us to pay for the water. She mumbled a few nice "compliments" in my direction and started to move on down the sidewalk towards the next group of runners. I was eventually able to help "Tinkerbell" arrive safely to a medical tent. Ironically, one of her friends had stopped there to wait for her because she had started to feel guilty for leaving her behind in the first place.

I paused for just a second to try to regain my energy and composure before moving on towards the finish line. I was in shock as the events of the day started to play back in my mind. I realized in the last few miles that I was not going to be able to contain my emotions. I was exhausted, frustrated and terribly disappointed in my performance during the race. I was ready to quit. I seriously considered the idea of just sitting down on the sidewalk and calling Rick to come and pick me up. I couldn't see the finish line. I didn't care about the medal that was going to be hung around my neck in just a few minutes. I wasn't bothered by the fact that my children would see that I quit so close to the finish line. My heart wasn't in this any longer and I couldn't clear my mind to remember why I was even doing it in the first place. My dream was being overshadowed by all of the circumstances that had disrupted my plans and corrupted my vision for the day. I was discouraged and done. Quitting was a real possibility now. I had convinced myself that no one would question my reasoning for quitting at this point. Most people would have quit when the blisters had started to burn at mile eleven.

The tears began to well up in my eyes and I begged God to give me just enough strength and determination to make it across the finish line. I desperately didn't want to quit yet another "thing" when I was so close to finishing it. I knew that I would not go on to finish the last six races if I stopped now. That's when God brought to mind a phrase that I had heard many times since starting my own business. It was something that my friend, Jordan, would say to encourage us while pursuing our entrepreneurial dreams. He would remind us that we should never quit on a bad day. Well this was the epitome of bad days for me. In my weary mind, I had to hold on to this phrase and just repeat it over and over as I put one foot in front of the other. Then I started to repeat 2 Timothy 4:7 to myself which is where Paul writes, "I have fought the good fight, I have finished the race, I have kept the faith." In this situation, it was exactly what I needed to repeat to myself to help me make it across that finish line. As I got closer and started to see the crowds around the finisher's area, I alternated between Jordan's instruction to never quit on a bad day with Paul's letter of encouragement to Timothy. I've always believed that God uses what moves us. In this moment, He certainly did that for me.

At that point, I was doing whatever I could to stay upright and not have to be carried out on a stretcher. I'm just so thankful that God gave me those two sources of inspiration. They took my mind off of myself and put them on the end goal of finishing this race strong. As I crossed the finish line and received my medal, I heard someone call my name. I looked over and saw my friend Cynthia from San Diego and her mom, Gwen. I was overwhelmed with gratitude that they chose to surprise me at the finish line. Gwen had been very ill, so I felt especially blessed that she would take the time to join Cynthia in support of my race challenge. I suddenly forgot about all of the obstacles and craziness of my day. Soon thereafter, Rick and the kiddos rescued me with all of the items that I had pre-ordered over the phone. We posed for our usual finish line photos, had our "this is why Mommy is working so hard" discussion and then loaded up the car to go home. As I started to re-tell the stories of my day, I had to field questions from my children on why I chose to keep going. It didn't make sense to them that I would continue after my feet were so badly blistered. They enjoyed hearing about "Tinkerbell" and the magic tonic water. As I shared the details and listened to the reactions from my family, I realized that God had given me plenty of opportunities that day to trust Him and grow deeper in my faith. I was also given the opportunity to see the strength that I had been given to continue, even when I wanted nothing more than to quit. I was able to share many of the lessons with my children in hopes that they would someday view challenges as opportunities. We all learned a lot from such a difficult experience. Specifically, we were convinced that we should never quit on a bad day.

As with all good lessons, this one crosses into other areas of my life as well. In ministry, I often get discouraged with people, especially myself. I see and hear things that make me want to kick, scream, cry and quit. I want people to know true joy and experience the peace that comes from knowing God personally. I want them to stop making life so difficult for themselves, their family members and friends. However, I understand that ministry is hard. It's messy and filled with lots of disappointments and frustrations. I've experienced much of that on a personal level and I grieve when I see others going through similar situations that I have endured in the past. One thing I know is that quitting is not an option in this area of my life. The apostle Paul, who sat in a dark Roman prison cell near the end of his life, wrote to Timothy to encourage him to keep the faith and finish the race. That's what I want to do as well, in all areas of life.

In business, I often have conversations with other entrepreneurs who are questioning whether or not to go on in their endeavors. I try to help them understand that they too can see the opportunities that come from challenges, if they simply choose to stay in the race. Without challenges, the rewards aren't quite as sweet when entrepreneurs reach their dreams. It almost feels like the journey isn't worth it if there aren't a few obstacles along the way. When a person reaches their goals professionally, others have the tendency to label them as "lucky". It's unfortunate that they don't have a "behind the scenes" look at the hard work, determination and faith that it took for that individual to be successful. My hope is that people will realize that everyone has a story that is filled with challenges and difficulties. The difference comes when we seize them as opportunities to learn, grow and thrive.

I pray that whenever I encounter someone who is ready to give up on their dreams, faith, business, or possibly even their life; God will give me the exact words and actions that will inspire them to keep going. Challenges come. They are hard. They sometimes hurt and make us feel as though we can't go on for one more second. But time passes and so do the challenges. Most often they are eventually revealed to be opportunities that grow us in ways that will radically change our lives and ultimately bless others in the process. I challenge you to continually be on the lookout for those opportunities.

Race #6 – A reminder to never quit on a bad day.
Phoenix Marathon
March 2013

I lift up my eyes to the hills. From where does my help come? My help comes from the Lord, who made heaven and earth.

-Psalm 121:1-2

Lesson #6:

Ask for Help

When I first started to focus on my race challenge, I realized quickly that this was not going to be an easy or simple endeavor. I had so many questions. I lacked much of the knowledge I would need to run such long distances, month after month. I needed help with nutrition, training and so much more. I began to look for the "experts". I wasn't necessarily searching for someone with a particular degree or a long title after their name. I was looking for those people who had gone before me in certain areas and could speak into the journey that I was about to take. For me, experts are the ones with real-life experience. I wanted and needed to surround myself with a support team that would be willing to help me along the way to achieve this seemingly impossible goal. Fortunately, God provided the perfect group of people that would literally and figuratively walk, jog and run every step with me. I was so thankful that I asked for help and was met with nothing but motivation and inspiration from everyone who was closely involved in my big adventure.

In the beginning, I started asking for prayer. I knew that Rick would be praying for me throughout the challenge. He knows my weaknesses and knows exactly what to ask God for when it comes to my struggles. My best friend, Faith, was also a prayer warrior on my behalf. Even though she didn't go to any of my races until number twelve, I always knew that she was with me in spirit and in prayer. Her support and encouragement during this year was a blessing that can't be easily described. The pastors and elders at my church also prayed for me. This meant a lot because these men were my shepherds, co-workers and friends. The fact that they were so supportive throughout my challenge just affirmed what I already knew. I work with a great group of guys who are my brothers in Christ.

Jason, my neighbor and friend, was a tremendous source of support and inspiration regarding the subject of running. He gave me tips that helped me to run faster and longer than I ever had before. He gave me the idea of not running with music so that I could enjoy the motivating sounds that come from being on a race course for hours with other like-minded people who were chasing their own goals. Jason also loaned me one of his running shirts which eventually became known as my "lucky shirt". His wife, Mandi, kept me on track with my nutritional needs. She sat for hours with me, discussing the best foods and supplements to consume to keep me healthy for the twelve months of the challenge. As a naturopathic doctor, she had all kinds of suggestions that helped me to stay in shape and injury-free.

As the long training miles started to take their toll on my body, I sought the help of my friend and chiropractor, Dr. Mike. Not only did he adjust my neck, back and shoulders, he offered additional training advice and suggestions. He thought up new ways to help me complete my next race with less pain. He helped improve my range of motion, flexibility and mental endurance for my events. I wouldn't have made it through the year of training and races if it weren't for Mike. He kept me going, both physically and emotionally. His tips and tricks were invaluable during the races in which I was battling one of many "war wounds" from my personal training days. I'm grateful that he was so willing to share his knowledge and experience in the area of fitness and chiropractic care. Along with Mike's adjustments, I would also seek the help of my massage therapist, Monica. She was able to help me recover from a race and prepare for the next one by working out all the problem areas that arose. I'm not sure if I benefited more mentally or physically from her massage therapy sessions. Whatever the case, I knew that her help was invaluable to my flexibility, joint pain relief and overall well-being.

The lesson of asking for help, even from strangers, played out in race number ten. The "Bucket of Blood" Half Marathon in Holbrook, Arizona was held on July 13, 2013. Because of the summer heat in Phoenix, I had to find a race somewhere in cooler temps. I went online and found this one that didn't seem to be too far of a drive. When I booked the race, I knew that it would be a different event for me because it would be my first trail run. Even so, I was ready for a new challenge and excited to get out of the scorching heat for a few days. Little did I know when I registered that I would have an even more difficult challenge during the race. Just two weeks before I was to run it, I discovered that I was pregnant. I was floored! At this time, I was forty-four years old. My husband and I had long since given up on the idea of having any more children of our own because of several miscarriages in the years prior. That fact was one of the reasons that we felt confident we were ready to become foster parents. In our hearts, we knew that we were done having our own children. We couldn't have been more wrong.

I checked in with my doctor and let him know about the pregnancy, as well as the race challenge. I was assured that since I had been running for so long that I should be fine to run the race. With that assurance, I headed north. I had mixed emotions that ranged from excitement to nervousness to loneliness because I had to do this race alone. Rick was working and no one else was available to go with me. The ride was peaceful and beautiful as I made my way through the pines of northern Arizona to a city that reminded me a lot of my hometown in Georgia. I spent much of the drive just thanking God for such an unexpected blessing. I now had a special secret that only Rick and I knew. After so many miscarriages, we were cautious not to tell anyone or get too excited until I made it through the first trimester. That evening, I enjoyed a quiet dinner alone and then gathered my race gear in preparation for the next day.

When the morning came, I got ready and walked up to the starting line alone. I felt an odd sensation in my stomach as I joined the other runners around a map that detailed the race course. I didn't know if it was my nerves or my newly pregnant body starting to revolt. As soon as I saw that I would mostly be running off-road in the surrounding mountain trails, I grew even more uneasy. Then, a conversation started about the woman who got lost on the course the previous year. I knew that I would be the one to get lost this time. I joked with one of the race coordinators that they might be out searching for me later since I didn't know the area and I only had experience running on paved roads. He assured me that I would be fine and that he would be on the lookout for me.

When the starting gun went off, I immediately felt something different from all of my other races. My legs felt heavy and tired. I had a nauseous feeling come over me and I realized that I was quickly becoming extremely emotional. This all took place before I ever completed the first mile. How was I going to get through the entire race if I felt this terrible already? I tried to calm myself down by meditating on a variety of quotes and Bible verses. It helped somewhat, but I knew that this was going to be a long and challenging race. As I tried to settle into my running pace, I realized that I was much slower than usual. I was working so hard to stay on the course and not get lost that I couldn't relax and enjoy the run. One by one, people were passing me. I was getting even more emotional as my pride took a huge beating. So much was going on in my head and body, all at the same time. I wondered if people could tell that I was ready to just sit down and cry. To make it worse, the directional arrows for the course were painted on the actual trail. Many of them had been destroyed by the feet of other runners ahead of me. By the time I got to them, they were mostly a blur of paint. Eventually, I just started following the bobbing heads in front of me on the desert trail. I felt sorry for myself and complained internally. Why was I there alone? Where were my friends and family? Had my support team completely disappeared? What if I got lost or injured? What if I got sick? I just needed someone to take my mind off of everything that seemed to be wrong. At that moment, the negativity had overtaken my thoughts and I was certain that things couldn't get any worse. As the frustration consumed me, I felt the knot in my stomach start to rise. Before I knew it, I was huddled over on the side of the trail, vomiting like never before. Great! Now I'm going to hurl my way through the next dozen miles! Why, God? What am I supposed to learn from this experience?

As I was cleaning myself off and trying to regain my desire to start running again, I begged God to provide some relief. I wanted clarity to determine if I should just hang up my shoes and use the pregnancy as an excuse to quit. I needed His help to make this decision. With tears in my eyes and vomit on my chin, I willed my feet to start moving. Just as I felt my rhythm coming back, I heard someone approaching me from behind. As I waited for yet another person to pass by and make me look as though I was running in slow motion, I realized that she had no intention of doing that. She actually started talking to me. She introduced herself as Rachel and asked a few questions about me and how I knew about this particular race. The conversation was light and easy, one that I could handle and run at the same time. I started to forget all the negative chatter in my head. For some reason, I eventually spit out the fact that I was pregnant. I think I wanted sympathy as well as a sense of security that someone else knew my secret. The next few miles rolled by with much more ease than the previous ones.

Eventually, I realized that Rachel was holding back on her pace to run alongside me. I told her to go ahead and not worry about me. I would be fine. I had actually started to believe it again. Once I gave her the permission to move on, she did just that. It was perfect timing because I soon found myself throwing up on the side of the road again. At this point, there were only a few people behind me on the course. They were much older than me so I had confidence that I could at least stay ahead of them and not be the last person to cross the finish line. I couldn't have been more wrong. After a few more "puke stops", I knew that I was the last runner as the senior citizens passed me up with ease. By this time, I had accepted the fact that this would be a slow, humbling race adventure. If I could get to the finish line at all, I would be happy. I continued on, trekking my way through the desert trails and country roads.

Since this was a small town race, there wasn't much support along the course. Whenever I did pass by one of the water stops, I had to fight the urge to ask for a ride to the finish line. I defaulted back to the idea that I couldn't quit on a bad day and that I had to finish the race that was set before me. At this point, I started to feel an odd sensation in my hands. I looked down to see that my fingers were swelling pretty quickly. My wedding band was disappearing under the skin that was stretching over it. When the numbness started to set in, I knew that I had to ask for help. At the next few pit stops, I asked for ice, but no one had any. I kept asking along the way and praying that there was no permanent damage happening in my hands. I remember asking God to protect me and my baby in that moment. In just a few minutes, He answered that prayer and sent help. A guy pulled up on an ATV and asked if I needed anything. When I showed him my hands and asked for ice, he offered to give me a ride to get help. For whatever reason, I turned down the ride and let him know that I would keep going on foot until he could return with the ice. After a few more miles, I accepted the fact that he must have forgotten about me. I held my hands over my head and tried to let gravity resolve the problem. It wasn't long before I heard someone pull up beside me and ask, "Do you still need that ice?" When I said yes, he tossed me a muddy Ziploc bag filled with actual square ice cubes. I was so desperate for the ice, I didn't care that the bag was muddy. However, I laughed at the thought that he must have gone home or shown up at someone else's house to raid their ice cube trays. I was blessed and overwhelmed with gratitude for this stranger and his willingness to help. With the ice in my hands, I started to move on towards the finish line.

At the next pit stop, a woman greeted me by name. She said, "Hey, Ellen. We've been waiting for you. How are you doing?" I was taken off guard by the fact that she knew me because I was certain that I didn't know anyone in Holbrook. She must have seen the look of surprise on my face because she then explained that she was Rachel's cousin. When Rachel passed by, she had asked her family to keep an eye out for me. I was touched, once again, by the compassion of strangers. At this point, I was beginning to see the light at the end of the tunnel. When my feet landed on the town streets again, I was relieved that at least I could wave down a car for help if I needed it. My guess was that I had less than a mile to go. That's when my heart sank. I saw Rachel running towards me. I knew that I must have gotten lost or off course. She had passed me many miles ago. She definitely shouldn't be running in my direction, so I knew that I must have gotten turned around in some way. I asked her how I could have gotten so messed up on the course. She shocked me with what she said next. "You aren't off course, Ellen. I came back from the finish line to get you so that you wouldn't cross it alone." It took a minute for me to even be able to respond. I started to thank her and express how touched I was that she came back for me. I also learned as we chatted that she herself hadn't crossed the finish line yet because she felt a prompting to do that with me. There just weren't words to express my gratitude for this woman and her selfless act of kindness.

How many people would sacrifice their own personal race time to go back for a stranger that they had just met for the very first time? I had not asked for Rachel's help, but she gave it freely. She saw and felt a need that she could meet, and she met it. What a selfless act on her part. Moments like this can only be from God as He works through the goodness in others. Together, we turned onto the last street that would take us to the end. I could see the finish line and all the people waiting for us. That's when I saw the guy who had delivered the ice cubes. He was there, waiting. He cheered me in, gave me my medal and received the sweaty, stinky hug that I would normally reserve for my family and close friends. I thanked him for helping me along the race course and asked his name. He let me know that he was glad to help and that his name was Lorin. Moments later, he dashed off to finish cleaning up the course signage and I never saw him again. Rachel eventually drifted into the crowd with her family and I just sat there, reliving all the events of the day. I couldn't believe that I had actually finished the race. I walked over to a place that was out of the way of the crowds, sat down and cried. I gratefully thanked God for all the ways that He had provided for me that day. I thanked Him for each person who helped me along the course, especially Rachel and Lorin. By being willing to ask for and receive help during this challenge, I was blessed to be covered in the "fingerprints" of many caring people. Some of them I knew. Some of them were strangers. Regardless, they were on the course with me, every step of the way. While contemplating this idea of helping people through the sharing of ideas, talents and experiences, I was reminded that I have also been given the opportunity to do this for others.

Over the years, I have met with people on a regular basis to discuss their desire to become foster parents. I don't consider myself to be an expert, but I do have knowledge and real-life experience that I can share with others in their journey to help children in need. The conversations I have with prospective foster parents are almost always the same set of questions which predominantly come from fear of the unknown. When I try to assure people that they can make a difference in the life of a child who needs them, I want them to realize that they don't have to be afraid because God already knows what is going to happen. They can choose faith over fear and rest in whatever direction He takes them. Now saying this is one thing. Living it is another.

Fortunately, my husband and I have been foster parents to six different children since getting licensed in 2011. We have experienced much heartache, but even greater blessings by being a part of the child welfare system in our state. When we counsel and encourage other families in this area, we usually have specific personal examples to share with them. We are living proof that you can survive, and thrive, in a situation where you choose to raise someone else's child at one of the most desperate times of their lives. We help others by sharing the pain and grief that we felt when our foster sons of two years were returned to their biological family. We also share the joy that we have in our hearts because their parents still remain in contact with us and allow visits with them from time to time. We don't just talk about this subject in theory. We've lived it and we want to help others step into this messy arena and make a difference along with us.

I have similar stories regarding adoption, both as an adoptive parent as well as an adopted child. I was adopted when I was eleven years old, after my biological mother died from colon cancer. Because of that traumatic experience, as well as the abuse I suffered at the hands of my step-father, I can share my thoughts from a survivor's vantage point. I can also give specific examples, from first-hand knowledge, of the pain and long term effects of being abused as a child and then being abandoned by the person who should have been my protector. I can also explain the relief that comes when another family makes the conscious decision to adopt a child who needs a home. I was that child. When I am asked to speak to a group about foster care or adoption, I help by sharing both the positive and negative sides of this subject. I give personal examples and tell my own story to help make the issues come alive and stay engrained in people's minds. I receive requests to meet when a person wants to hear about my experiences and hopefully draw strength and courage to follow God's calling in their lives to foster or adopt. When there is a need for encouragement in this area, they want to discuss it with someone who not only knows about the topic, but has lived it and can speak from their own experiences.

In ministry, I seek after the people who are more mature in Christ than me. They aren't always older than I am. They have just been walking longer with the Lord. As a single Christian many years ago, I would spend time with couples that I admired and trusted to share their experiences with me. I wanted to hear from them how life could be lived out in a way that would honor God and bless my spouse. I wanted them to share their struggles and their victories. Still today, I never look specifically for the person who knows the key Bible verses by heart, unless they also display them in their life. What they know in their head isn't as important to me as what they feel in their heart. I also look for the people who are putting their faith into action. They are the ones that are out in the world, seeking to make a difference, for the Kingdom of God. I need help from the people who have walked before me on the path that I'm on now and I watch for them. Fortunately, God is always faithful to bring them into my life.

In my business, I search for those who have gone before me in network marketing. I want to learn from them. Who better to teach me how to grow my business and benefit from the personal development aspects of our profession? Whenever I hear an expert teaching on a particular area of networking or business building, I take notes and then always wait for the story. It drives home the point of whatever they are teaching and reinforces their knowledge of this profession. If they only show me numbers and statistics, I'm not interested. I need the real-life examples from them, both good and bad. Down the road, I can refer back to their story and gain motivation from the fact that I know someone who has actually lived it. For this reason alone, in many areas of my life, I now ask for help from the experts.

Two of the kindest and most selfless people I know: Mandi and Jason Croniser, with their son, Gavin.

I love doing life with these ladies and learning something new every time we get together.
Faith Herrera and Mandy Curtis

I couldn't wait to get home to this cool kid ... my son, Peyton.
Race #10 - Bucket of Blood Half Marathon
July 2013

Lesson #7:

Increase Your Joy

There is a Swedish proverb that reads, "Shared sorrow is halved. Shared joy is doubled". I knew when I started this challenge that I wanted to include others on the journey. Adventures are always more fun when others are there to share them with us. When I began planning my races, I knew I had friends who were runners or aspiring runners. I knew people who liked to participate in any sort of physical challenge. I knew others who simply wanted to learn to dream again by watching me go through this process. Because of all these people, as well as my desire to never do it alone, I asked others to join me. I wanted them to go along for the doubled joy. They could run a race, be a part of my training, go to a race expo, be my traveling partner or participate in whatever way they would like to be involved. I wanted to have someone to share the trials as well as the celebrations with me. Fortunately for me, there were a few brave souls who even dared to lace up their shoes and commit to join me along the way.

My friend, Cynthia, was someone I met back in 2003 while I was planning my wedding in San Diego. I knew her brother and sister-in-law from my church in Arizona. They introduced us when they heard that Rick and I wanted to have a "destination wedding" in southern California. From the moment we met, I knew that Cynthia was my kind of gal. She was a marine and a police officer for the city of San Diego. She liked to travel, be adventurous and take on any sort of challenge we could throw her way. And that's what we did by asking her to help with our wedding plans. As soon as we mentioned our need for her input, she went to work. She found pretty much all of the contacts we needed to make our dream wedding a reality. We couldn't have asked for a better wedding weekend. We enjoyed a welcome party on the beach, a waterfront wedding on Island Point Lawn and a sunset reception with the ocean as our backdrop. It was perfect! Since that time, we have grown closer as friends. She has opened her home to us countless times over the last decade. She has been our chauffeur, chaperone, tour guide, babysitter, trip advisor and trusted confidante. She is a cherished part of our family. I can't imagine what our wedding, or our lives, would have been like without Cynthia being a part of them.

The same goes for my race challenge. She was instrumental in keeping me motivated. Whether it was with a phone call, text or face-to-face chat, Cynthia knew how to inspire me to just go for it. She had a different sort of motivation than most. Usually she would make some joke about how she would probably be crawling on the course or how I might have to carry her home after the race. In her own funny way, Cynthia made me believe that I could do anything I set my mind to do. Better than just encouraging me with her words, she chose to motivate me with her presence by running a couple of the races with me. Those were some of my favorite times during the challenge.

Race number five was the Women's Half Marathon in San Diego on February 24, 2013. It was a great race, from start to finish. The weather was perfectly cool and sunny, as you would expect from southern California. My family was with me for this one, which meant a lot. Having Cynthia run the race made it even better. When Rick dropped us off at the starting area early that morning, Cynthia immediately began with her usual jokes and light-hearted sarcasm. She kept me smiling while we waited in the long porta potty line and then calmed my nerves as we crammed into the packed corral for a delayed start. I was beginning to get anxious during the delay, but Cynthia easily took my thoughts elsewhere by planning how we could make it even better next year. She suggested we sleep an extra hour and just find a better drop off point to reduce our wait time in the corral. She was figuring out the best streets for us to use as well as other details that would make it smoother and even more fun for us in the future. I like that about her. She is always thinking about and planning her next big adventure.

When the race started, we eventually parted ways as our individual paces were different. That didn't bother either one of us.

We just came to run. At the finish line, we reunited and celebrated by hanging out on the grass, taking photos and laughing at the endless jokes and stories that Cynthia had from the race. I loved that she had fun and could laugh at herself. She would deflect my positive comments about her with yet another self-deprecating joke, but I knew that she was proud to have finished the race. After that, we were off to celebrate our accomplishments with a post-race breakfast at Tobeys 19th Hole Restaurant. It was a small "mom and pop" place, located on a golf course. The restaurant itself was relatively small and had a very casual environment. From the outside, you'd never guess what you would see once you entered the dining area. There was a large window that provided a spectacular view of the golf course as well as the city skyline. It was the perfect setting for us to enjoy our post-race breakfast and share some of the event highlights with my family. Memories like these last for a lifetime and I'm so grateful that I had special people there with me to celebrate.

Race number nine was a little different experience in San Diego. It was the P.F. Chang's Rock 'n' Roll Marathon on June 2, 2013. It happened to fall on the same weekend as the national convention for my network marketing company, which was in Salt Lake City that year. Because of the different locations, I had to do some extra planning to be able to run in southern California. On the last day of convention, I had to leave a few hours early in order to get to the airport. I hopped on a flight from Salt Lake to San Diego with plans to arrive in time to pick up my race packet before the expo closed at 5:00pm. If I didn't pick it up by that time, I would be unable to run the next morning. When I arrived in San Diego, Cynthia was waiting for me curbside to drive me to the convention center before it closed. She had already told me that she didn't feel ready to run in this race, but that she would be there to support me during the process. As we drove towards the expo, I made my best attempts to convince her to run, despite her lack of training to prepare. I even assured her that I would have a harder time on this race because I had just run race number eight, which was a half marathon, only five days earlier in Utah.

As we approached the convention center, we realized quickly that I might not make it in time to pick up my race packet. Traffic in San Diego was sitting at a standstill due to all the out-of-town participants who were trying to make their way into the expo. Cynthia passed the time and calmed my nerves by making jokes about not being ready or able to run in the race. Eventually, I convinced her to at least pick up her packet, just in case she changed her mind. We finally made it to the expo, grabbed our race bibs and swag bags, and then headed back to the car. We spent the next hour sitting in traffic in the underground parking structure of the building. We joked about running out of gas for a while, then started contemplating the fact that we might be sleeping there for the night. We imagined all the funny scenarios that could take place if traffic didn't start moving soon. We even joked that all the exhaust fumes were going to be the end of us, then and there.

Once we finally saw daylight again, we headed out for some good carbs, many more jokes and lots of laughter. By the time we were getting ready for bed, I had finally convinced her to do the half marathon route. We decided to meet up after I finished the marathon and celebrate together. After we crossed the starting line, I didn't see Cynthia again until several hours later. She had already finished the race, gone home, showered and come back for me at the finish line. Now that's a friend! We continued our tradition of a post-race celebration and breakfast at Tobeys. We swapped race stories, laughed about all the craziness of the day and then went home to sleep it off. I can't imagine my races in San Diego without Cynthia. She made every one of them fun, special and incredibly memorable.

In ministry, I have been able to find ways that I can help others in their desire to grow in their walk with the Lord. Ultimately, by doing so, they will experience a joy that can only come from knowing Him. The primary role of my current ministry position is to help others grow in their faith and connect to our congregation in a variety of ways. Whether I am connecting newcomers to a particular small group, service ministry or class, I try to remember the importance of doing things with a "team" mentality. Life is hard.

Ministry is hard. Relationships are hard. However, when we join others on the journey, we can help carry one another's burdens. We can also share in their joy. One of my favorite ways to do this is through small group settings or community groups. People need people. They need face-to-face interaction and accountability. With community groups, we can make a big church seem small. Meeting weekly with other like-minded individuals is encouragement for the soul. When times are difficult or painful, we grieve with them. When things are going great for someone, we rejoice with them. Seeing God work through people to bless others is such a privilege for me.

In my business, I enjoy seeing the various teams develop throughout our organization. In the end, we are all one big team. However, the support and inspiration that comes from working with like-minded colleagues can mean the difference between quitting and persevering. As often as possible, I like to arrange gatherings of different team members. Through these opportunities, we can share our wisdom and experience to help others who are on the same journey to financial and time freedom. As a part of a team, events and getaways are also more enjoyable. More importantly, it's a true blessing to celebrate when someone reaches another milestone in their business or sees how they are impacting others in a positive way through their endeavors.

Looking back over the past several years and thinking about our family's exponential growth, I know that we wouldn't have made it without the people who God placed in our lives. From the moment we became foster parents until the day we heard the judge's final declaration of adoption, we were incredibly blessed with people who were willing to step onto the path with us. Often times, it was a very messy road that they chose. When we would get sidelined by odd behaviors or irrational actions from our foster children, someone would step in with words of wisdom and scriptures to help us have an eternal perspective on what was actually happening in our home. Sometimes it would be a simple text, call or message that would take us from despair and frustration back to dependence and trust in God to handle the situation. Our church family and friends were instrumental in keeping our eyes on whatever the Lord might have been doing through the various challenges and struggles that came our way through the foster care system. Several times, we received unexpected gifts of food, supplies, diapers and cleaning products on our doorstep. At other times, we would be given the opportunity to have a date night when someone would be brave enough to step in and care for our seven children. We are eternally grateful for each and every person who God used to increase our joy through their generosity, love and compassion.

Doubled joy with Cynthia Hanna
Race #5 - San Diego Women's Half Marathon
February 2013

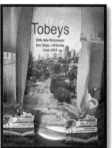

Post-race celebration breakfast at Tobeys
Race #9 - P.F. Chang's Rock 'n' Roll Marathon
June 2013

Lesson #8:

Join the Thirteen Percent

At my first network marketing event, I was taught the 87/13 statistic which states that 87% of the things that impact us in our daily lives is negative. That negativity comes from many different sources, both internal and external. Our minds naturally tend to drift towards the negative side of any situation. We have to work hard to counteract the barrage of outside influences upon our emotions, thinking and behavior. Newspapers, magazines, television, social media, emails, texts and the gossip from people in our lives all join together to keep us informed on the worst case scenarios of life. It's a constant battle to draw ourselves away from the "dark side" and focus on the good things in life. I've always said that I'd like to see a television show that only focused on the good news of the day. However, I realize that it probably wouldn't be successful because that's not the type of news that sells. It's a sad situation.

There have been countless studies done to prove that focusing on the positive things in life will help us live longer and experience a greater degree of contentment and happiness. By being in a positive environment, we live longer, experience better health, greater wealth and more success in our careers. In several articles I have read over the past few years, positivity can benefit us mentally, emotionally, spiritually, physically and financially. As soon as I started to see the difference that comes from living in a positive environment, I chose to join the 13%.

During my race challenge, I had to intentionally remove myself from negative people, conversations and situations. I was fortunate that we had stopped watching regular TV programming about a year before I started to run my races. The day we stopped our cable television service would prove to be one that changed our family dynamics forever. We found that we had more time together, more productive days and a more positive environment in our home. We talked more, played more and enjoyed fun activities with one another. Having such an enjoyable home life impacted my training, nutrition and overall race performance. I even set up some unofficial "experiments" on the treadmill at my gym. I would test my emotions and energy levels while watching a news show one day and then do the same test while watching something inspiring and uplifting, such as a movie with a positive theme. Without fail, my training runs were always better when I had a motivating source of entertainment. For that reason, I chose to limit my environment as best I could to ones that were positive, energetic and inspiring. I encourage you to do the same type of test. Try spending a specific amount of time in your day with the news playing on your TV. Monitor your emotions and your mood as you hear about all the horrible things that go on, moment by moment, in our world. Then, on a different day, spend the same amount of time listening to encouraging music. Whatever genre motivates and uplifts you, play it for the same amount of time that you watched TV previously. Again, take note of your emotions and reactions. I'd love to hear what you learn from such an easy, yet impactful experiment.

I can compare races within the challenge and see how this 87/13 statistic was involved. For example, the Phoenix Marathon that I previously described in detail was a near impossible event for me. It started with the stressful morning in traffic and didn't improve significantly until I crossed the finish line. On the contrary, my race in San Francisco was filled with the motivating enthusiasm of my friend, Laura. The race was smooth and enjoyable because I was surrounded with spectacular views, encouraging people and many positive influences. There were other races that fell on the spectrum between these two polar opposite experiences. In those, I had to simply exercise my ability to look towards the positive and not drift to the negative aspects of any situation. That ability came as I meditated on one particular verse from scripture.

Philippians 4:8 reads, " Finally, brothers, whatever is true, whatever is honorable, whatever is just, whatever is pure, whatever is lovely, whatever is commendable, if there is any excellence, if there is anything worthy of praise, think about these things." I had learned this from a message taught to my singles' group back in my early days as a Christian. The teaching pastor, Larry, told us that he and his family would encourage each other in times of difficulty by saying, "We need to Philippians 4:8 the situation". That phrase stuck with me and I repeat it often as I walk through my daily life, being bombarded by the 87%.

Please understand that I am not trying to live in a bubble or avoid the incredible difficulties that are a part of life. I simply choose, by God's grace, not to let challenges rob me of my joy or affect how I see certain situations. I also choose to proactively do my part to impact the world in a more positive way. Personally, I know the feeling of being paralyzed by fear, anxiety and depression. I have experienced the pain and suffering that comes from being abandoned by a parent. I know the heartache that comes from a failed marriage. I have grieved the loss of several children through miscarriages. I also see injustices that occur all around me on a daily basis. However, I choose to see the good that can come from these situations as the Lord works through people to help others. Complaining about the injustices of our day doesn't change them. Prayer and action leads to change. By positioning my focus on the positive outcome that can result, I don't remain in a state of apathy. I believe that God either allows or causes all things to happen for a reason. Even though I might not know why, I do trust that it is all part of His great plan for my life and others. I only wish that I would have known this truth many years ago when I would allow the 87% in life to completely sideline me for long periods of time.

Ironically, I can easily be affected by the difficulties that come from being in a full-time ministry position at church. I still remember the first day that I started working for a church and realized that it's not all grassy meadows and sunshine behind-the-scenes. Christians are human, like everyone else. We sin, make mistakes and experience conflict. We offend one another, say the wrong things sometimes and forget to express our gratitude to others. Unfortunately, these simple facts that apply to all humans are what many people use to criticize Christians. However, there is one word that serves as my reminder to focus on the good. That word is "grace". I received it when God chose to open my eyes to what Jesus did for me on the cross. I receive it daily from others who have an eternal perspective and choose to see what God is doing through a difficult situation. God is working among us. He is moving. He is using our struggles and the negative circumstances in our world to point us back to Him.

By choosing to be a network marketing professional, I automatically place myself in the cross hairs of a negative scope. Many people, because of past experiences or a simple lack of knowledge, have a negative opinion of the profession. I understand that someone's experience with a "bad" network marketer may influence their view of the business model. However, I don't feel that it's a reason to stereotype those of us who are working hard to elevate the profession and bless others through our businesses. I personally know people who have become very successful in network marketing and have coached others to do the same along the way. Many of these successful entrepreneurs provide resources and funding to charitable organizations, ministries and missionaries. Others have built orphanages and rescue organizations around the world. Because of the business model and residual income that is part of it, people can achieve financial freedom and enjoy more time to do what really matters to them. Ultimately, they are able to spend more of their days helping others. Like any profession, there are great people involved, as well as some not-so-great people. I choose to focus on the positive success stories that empower and inspire me to live a generous life as I help others in the process. By doing so, I can remain a part of the 13% and hopefully inspire those around me to do the same.

Lesson #9:

Share Your Story

Throughout this book, I use the word "share" a lot. I refer to sharing our time, energy, resources, knowledge and experiences. I fully believe that we aren't meant to keep all of this to ourselves. We are created to help others by living a generous life and sharing it. One of the best ways that I have found to do this is to tell stories. Storytelling is an art form, but it doesn't have to be difficult. The stories just need to be true and told from the heart. As I began to share my goal of running twelve races, I heard lots of stories from runners of all ability levels. Their stories, as well as the wisdom that was gained from them, inspired me to keep going with my own training. I was encouraged by the adventures that others had enjoyed while running, but I also avoided a lot of mistakes because I listened to the wisdom of those who had gone before me on the path.

While discussing my self-imposed race challenge, people would also ask for the story behind it. They wanted to know why I would ever set such a lofty goal, knowing how busy I was with my family, job at the church, network marketing business, homeschooling and parenting. I would respond with my story about the first convention I ever attended and what I had learned about the "I Am" statement. Once I started the challenge, I would have even more stories to tell after crossing the finish line of yet another race. Prior to 2012, I don't remember feeling like I had a story to share. I know now that I had plenty to tell, but I certainly didn't understand the importance of sharing it. Over time, I noticed how people were often asking me to share my other stories with them. Because of my involvement in the 90 Day Tithe Challenge, I was asked for the steps that we took to become financially free from debt. I would also be asked about my involvement in foster care or what it was like to homeschool my children. Other times, I was questioned about my business and the personal development side of it. Through these situations, I began to notice that I was always telling a story of some sort. I realized that I enjoyed sharing my experiences with others, even when the stories might have been extremely painful. However, I knew that sometimes those most difficult stories would inspire others to step out in faith and try something new.

For example, after race number seven in San Francisco, I returned home to a voice mail message from our foster care case manager that felt like a punch to the stomach. She was calling to inform me that our foster sons would be returning home to their biological parents that week. This came as a total surprise because we had already been told that we would most likely be able to adopt them. There was no forewarning of this change back to reunification and we only had a few days to explain it to our sons, pack their belongings and return them to their previous home. Our family was devastated. We had raised and cared for these boys for two years. It was especially challenging, but truly rewarding. We experienced first words, first steps, first swimming lessons and first visits to the beach. We saw them grow, improve and become well-mannered, emotionally stable children who knew that they were in a safe and secure home. In just one phone call, our family's story was about to change and our boys would be leaving us. I was told to be in court the next day for the final ruling and return of our sons. I was in complete shock and couldn't gain control of my sudden outbursts of anger, frustration and sadness as I prepared to leave for the hearing. The tears would just start rolling down my face uncontrollably. I walked into court, feeling as if "the system" had completely wronged our boys, as well as our family.

After the final judgment was made, I begged for just a few more days with our sons before we had to return them to their biological family. We knew that the boys would be confused by the sudden and unexpected changes. We hoped for at least a few days to discuss everything with them and explain that we would always love them. We wanted them to fully understand that they would always have our hearts, even if they didn't have our name. Their parents agreed to give us a few extra days so that we could have those discussions and also pack all of the things that so many people had given our sons over the two years that they lived with us.

My heart was breaking as I tried to explain the details to our own biological children, as well as our foster sons. I wanted desperately to put my own selfish desires aside and just love unconditionally since we were obviously meant to be a part of the reunification of this family. I went through moments of weakness when I imagined ways that we could disappear with the boys and our family. How could we prevent this reunification? I couldn't fathom our lives without our sons. We had invested so much time and energy into their lives. Harder still, were the discussions with my biological children and how much they would miss their brothers. Because of my own grief and frustration over the situation, I found it hard to trust whatever it was that God was teaching us through this. All I knew was that I had to keep busy with other things to keep from going crazy with anxiety and stress. Fortunately for me, I worked for a church and Easter weekend was just a few days away. It was our second busiest season of the year, so I had plenty to do. Whenever possible, I would turn my focus to all of the events and details that needed to be handled for Good Friday and Easter Sunday. Sandwiched between those two days was what I now refer to as Reunification Saturday.

That morning, we loaded bin after bin into our van. We wanted to return our sons to their family with some extra clothing and supplies that would give them a good start back at home. Throughout the morning, I would bite my lip and try to hold back the tears as I hugged our boys again and again in an attempt to assure them that we would always be their mommy, daddy, sister and brother. Since day one in our home, that's how they had referred to us. But on this particular day of reunification, they would be going back to their first family. We had planned a "celebration" in the park, complete with lunch and play time. We had hoped that this would make for an easier transition for everyone involved. What I hadn't expected was how excited the boys were to return home. For some prideful reason, I just assumed that they would want to stay with us because of all that we had done for them and all the fun that they had experienced while in our care. As much as they loved us, it was obvious that they were returning to their home of choice. In some ways, it was very hurtful to watch how easily they integrated back into their birth family. On the other hand, it was truly a blessing for us to see such joy in their faces when they went back to their old room. They bounced on their beds and dug out their old toys that they hadn't seen in years. As we gave them our last goodbyes and lingering hugs, I knew that God had used us to help re-build a family, even when it felt like He was deconstructing ours.

The next day was Easter Sunday and I was responsible for helping behind-the-scenes with the baptisms of several of our church members. I stood backstage, watching first-hand and listening to stories about how God was changing lives. In those same moments, I was grieving in a way that was indescribable. I felt like something had died inside of me. If nothing else, my desire to foster was gone. I couldn't imagine going through this painful situation ever again. I was exhausted from the roller coaster of emotions that day as I rejoiced in what Jesus had done on the cross. But at the same time, I wondered what God was doing in my family. I wasn't sure that I could bear the pain that would occur if we went through a similar situation in the future. I questioned whether or not I could actually handle foster care, which was a scary place for me to be emotionally. For the two years prior, I had been speaking and teaching on how foster care was a ministry and how people could grow in their faith and obedience to God as they stepped into the messiness that came with helping children and families in need. Now I wasn't certain that I could assure people of that fact because I was desperately hurting.

I didn't have much time to consider the option of leaving foster care because our phone rang the very next day with a request for us to take in two young girls. I agreed to take them, without even considering the pain that I was still experiencing over the return of our boys. I can look back now and see that I was on auto-pilot for quite a while with our girls. I loved and cared for them. I made sure that they were happy and secure. However, I didn't let my guard down as quickly as I had with our boys. I knew that I was still grieving and I could see that others in my family were doing the same. It looked different in each of our lives, but it was still obvious to us that we needed time to readjust and move past the pain we were feeling.

Then, in late summer, relief came in the form of a voice mail message. Even though the biological parents had agreed to let us see our boys after they returned home, we had not yet been given that opportunity. When we had offered to make the trip to their side of town for a visit, we were told that the boys needed more time to get settled back into their home. I had begun to think that our fear of never seeing them again was going to come true. When I saw that I had missed a call from their mom, I initially panicked. I was concerned that maybe something bad had happened. Instead, I listened to the voice mail message and felt the tears begin to stream down my cheeks. The boys' mother had called to let me know that it was the first day of school for one of our sons and that she knew he would want to speak to his mommy on such a special day. To hear her call me his mommy was simply too much for me to handle in that moment. Immediately, I felt that God was giving me the answer to a question that I had asked many times over the past few years, and especially during the past several months. I wondered if we had made a difference, left an impact or had any influence whatsoever on their lives. They were so young when they came to live with us. Would they even remember us? My answers came that day, in a very short voice mail message. In the weeks after that, we were able to celebrate birthdays and enjoy some time with our boys. It brought us all relief to see them, to know that they were okay, and that we were still their family.

This is the story I share when I meet people who are interested in foster care, but are concerned that they might not be able to handle it when their foster children are returned to the families from which they were taken initially. I can now say, without hesitation, that being a foster parent is difficult, challenging and painful when the children are reunified with their parents. However, I can also say that it is all worth it when God puts a family back together and uses ordinary people like us to make it happen. Grief subsides.

Pain lessens. Lives change. Families reunite. We get to be a part of it all and that's an incredible privilege and blessing.

In ministry, stories are a given. Testimonies, or "God stories", are so common that they are often overlooked until someone needs to be encouraged. We can share, through the work that God has done in our own hearts, how life can be full of love, joy, peace, patience, kindness, goodness, gentleness, faithfulness and self-control. I have spent countless hours listening to the stories that others have shared about their faith in Christ. I've also heard the stories about life before they became a Christian. Baptism stories are some of the best. I am always inspired when I hear how someone has gone from sadness, despair and hopelessness to a life lived in the freedom of Christ. There's nothing, absolutely nothing, compared to it. Rick and I have been able to share many of our own God stories to magnify the Lord and what He has done in our family through foster care and adoption. We also share our story of going from bankruptcy in the early years of our marriage to financial freedom through the 90-Day Tithe Challenge. Our goal is always to point people back to Christ and impress upon them that they too can do all things through His strength. It simply takes a moment of decision when they choose their faith over the fear that can keep them from realizing true joy and fulfillment.

When I first started my business, I enjoyed hearing the stories that people shared. Some would involve personal development and others described financial success. I especially liked to hear the triumphant, "rags to riches" stories. They appealed to me because they demonstrated what can happen with faith, hard work, perseverance and determination. The stories often revealed something miraculous that God had done in someone's life because of their business. I've listened to many different speakers share how their lives have been changed by their network marketing business and the personal development that accompanies it. The training in network marketing is some of the best I've ever experienced because it makes us look at how we can grow and improve in order to enjoy a more fulfilling life as we help others in the process. So much of it is common sense when you consider the actual teaching. It's simply a matter of applying the virtues of kindness, generosity and encouragement to our business and personal relationships.

Being a foster parent is not easy,
but it is worth it.

Celebrating with my family ... priceless!
Race #8 - Memorial Day Classic Half Marathon
May 2013

"As we express our gratitude, we must never forget that the highest appreciation is not to utter words, but to live by them."

-John F. Kennedy

Lesson #10:

Express Your Gratitude

Notice that the title of this chapter is not "Be Grateful". When asked if they are grateful, most people will say yes. Besides, who wants to admit that they are ungrateful? However, there is a big difference between being grateful and actually expressing that gratitude. I learned the importance of this while attending my first network marketing convention back in 2012. One of the distributors with our company introduced us to something called The 30-Day Gratitude Challenge. It was a genius idea and I immediately knew that I had to participate. The concept was very simple. Jeff challenged us to think of someone each day, for thirty days, that we appreciate. Then, we would take the next step to express our gratitude by sending a card to let the recipient know that we appreciated them. I couldn't wait to get started. During a break, I snuck off to my hotel room to send my first card. I sent it to my husband. In just a matter of minutes, I had expressed my sincere love, respect and gratitude for him in a card. That one card made such an impact on him. He still has it now, several years later.

By participating in this challenge, I not only saw how much it touched others in a positive way, but I could also see and feel how it was affecting me personally. I spent time each morning thanking God for a particular individual and then sat down to send them a heartfelt card of gratitude. It was a fantastic way to begin each day. It turned my focus to the blessings in my life and kept my attention where it should be: on God and others. After about a week, I started to receive responses from people who had been the recipients of my cards. I was surprised at how much they were touched by receiving such a simple gesture of kindness. I soon realized that the lack of gratitude expression needed to be changed. People should hear that they are appreciated. It needed to be something tangible that they could hold, keep and re-read when they are hurting or feeling overlooked. Later, I would see my cards in the homes of friends, offices of different businesses that I used, and hanging on walls of restaurants where I dined. It was pretty cool to think that I could encourage people in such a simple way.

During the race challenge, I was especially focused on expressing my gratitude. As a matter of fact, I spent many miles along my race routes thanking God for the endless blessings in my life. I would thank Him for each individual person or thing that came to mind as I thought through my on-going gratitude lists. Surprisingly, as I did this, my runs felt much easier because my mood was lifted. So many people had helped me along the way and I gave all glory to God for how He brought each of them as a gift along my journey. Furthermore, I knew that I needed to reach out to everyone that the Lord had placed in my path during the year-long challenge. After each race, I made a list of the people who were involved and sent them a card. Many times, I also sent a gift to express how much I appreciated them for making my race experience a great one.

One particular instance occurred when I went into an athletic wear store to buy a pair of running pants. The salesperson was an extremely outgoing and congenial woman. She quickly asked my name and how she could assist me. She spent the next half hour helping me to find just the right pair of pants for my needs. She referred to me by name and continued to bring items to the dressing room for me to try on so that I didn't have to go back and forth. She was honest with her feedback about the pants I tried. She was also unbelievably encouraging throughout the process. Since I didn't have the stereotypical marathoner's body shape, it was no easy task to find the perfect pants. However, she did it and I was out the door with my new compression running gear. My next race time proved that those pants were the ones I needed. In just one race, I shaved fourteen minutes off of my overall half marathon time. That's unheard of in most running circles. I was so thankful for such a wonderful experience that I created a card that had my finish line photo and the logo of the store on it. I thanked the salesperson by name in my card and sent it off to the company. It felt really great to have the chance to thank her and recognize her outstanding customer service skills.

Several months later, I decided to stop by that store again to see if I could buy a sports bra that was made from the same material as my pants. I walked in with my hopes set on working with the same salesperson. Unfortunately, she wasn't there, but the manager helped me in much the same way as I had experienced previously when I bought the pants. Before I left, I asked if the original woman still worked there, only to find out that she had transferred to a different store. I briefly mentioned to the manager that the woman had been an incredible help when I was looking for my compression pants. As soon as I said this, the manager pointed at me and asked, "Aren't you the runner who sent us the cool, personalized card?" When I told her that it was me, she motioned for me to follow her over to the back office door. She pointed inside to my card that was hanging above her desk. I was shocked and blessed to see it hanging there. When I mentioned that I had sent it to the saleslady that had helped me months earlier, the manager assured me that a copy had been sent to the other store for her. However, the manager wanted to keep the card in her office as a reminder that some people do take the time to appreciate excellent service. She said that she showed it to other employees to encourage them that outstanding service really does matter. Unfortunately, her experience was that most people only take the time to write a letter when they are upset or disappointed in their service experience. She told me that my card had served as a source of motivation for her and others to continue to do their best. By seeing it hanging there on the wall, they would be reminded that people do appreciate the employees' efforts, even when it isn't always expressed in writing.

I was so thankful to see that something as simple as a card could impact more than just the intended recipient. I realized then that I would spend the rest of my life recognizing people for the ways that they love, serve and support others. I also knew that I would make it my mission to help others understand the importance of expressing gratitude. By doing so, we could collectively change the world. I believed that fact with all my heart then, and still do today. I decided to first focus on gratitude at home with my own family. To see my husband and children sending cards of appreciation has affected me in so many ways. We spend time each week, picking people that we want to bless with our words of thankfulness. My children choose their teachers, friends from church, neighbors and many others to bless with their cards. We have sent cards and gifts to foster care case workers, licensing agency representatives, lawyers, judges and many more. They are part of a system that can be terribly discouraging. For that reason, we want to do our part to inspire them to keep going. When our foster sons were returned home, we dealt with our grief by focusing on all the blessings that came from that situation. We sent cards and brownies to everyone involved in our case. Some of the recipients reached out to us to say how much they were touched to receive our cards and gifts. It is still my prayer that they will remember those cards and realize just how much their work is appreciated, especially in the tougher situations when it seems that no one cares about the difficulties of living in a world of red tape.

As a staff member in full-time ministry, I can see how expressing gratitude grows our horizontal relationships with others. Better than that, our vertical relationship with God skyrockets as we focus on the blessings that He rains down upon us and the people that He uses to bless us. A culture of appreciation is a fierce one in the battle against pride, selfishness and negativity. It's contagious when people begin to send and receive words of encouragement and gratitude. We can't go wrong by expressing our thankfulness to God and others. Nothing but good can come from it, so I will spend the rest of my days choosing to bless others by appreciating them and teaching others to do the same.

In my business, I have been able to enjoy the rewards of thanking others and letting them know how much I appreciate them for remaining loyal to our company. I love using my own company's product as a way to bless others through gratitude. I'm now taking it to a different level by showing other business owners how they can do the same. As entrepreneurs learn the value of appreciating their customers, transactions turn into relationships. When medical professionals reach out to their patients in gratitude, they go from being doctors to caregivers. In non-profit organizations, leaders can now make their volunteers feel like family. What's fun for me is to hear the stories that roll in approximately one week after the cards of gratitude are sent. The recipients are blessed. The senders are blessed. It's a win-win situation.

> *Gratitude is not only the greatest of virtues, but the parent of all the others.*
>
> *-Marcus Tullius Cicero*

Special thanks to the students of my inaugural class, "GRATITUDE: The Missing Link" at Redemption Gateway church. I've been blessed to see God work in and through each of you as you've reached out to others in love, compassion and gratitude. -Ellen

For I know the plans I have for you," declares the Lord, "plans to prosper you and not to harm you, plans to give you hope and a future.

-Jeremiah 29:11 (NIV)

Lesson #11:

Trust God's Plan

From the moment that I wrote the "I Am" statement regarding my race challenge, I had to grow in my faith and trust of God's plan. I had to choose to keep going each step of the way, even when I had no idea how I was going to accomplish my goal. There were times of loneliness when I wanted to quit. There were moments of discouragement when I questioned why I was even attempting such a crazy endeavor. There were days when I didn't want to train. On other days, I didn't want to eat as I knew I should. I would lose focus of my end goal and all the things that I could possibly learn from the journey. Then, God would give me a glimpse of victory through one more finish. He would put someone in my path that motivated me with their words and supportive actions. He would work out the details for my travel, hotel accommodations, race registrations and more. I was continually amazed at how He went before me to make things happen in some pretty miraculous ways. Whenever I faltered in my faith, He was always there, keeping my feet on the path and giving me direction on which way to go. He used countless individuals in this process to keep me moving forward. Ultimately, I was able to keep my eyes focused on the fact that I could trust Him above all else as I chased after my goals.

When I learned that I was pregnant just before race number ten, I found myself on a different sort of journey. To say that I was shocked is a huge understatement. Because of my age and several miscarriages, Rick and I had determined years earlier that it was time to move into the realm of foster care. We had accepted the fact that we weren't meant to have more children of our own and hadn't really discussed it for quite a while. However, as soon as we found out that I was expecting, we were overjoyed. We knew that we wouldn't tell others until I was at least finished with the first trimester because that's when all of our miscarriages had happened in the past.

After the initial excitement settled, we then had to discuss what to do about my races. We would do whatever God put on our hearts. It just didn't seem to be a clear decision for either of us. My first visit to the doctor made it easier to discuss and eventually decide that I would continue to run as long as I felt comfortable doing so. My doctor assured me that because I had been running so much prior to the pregnancy that I should be fine to continue. After checking my blood pressure, heart rate and other health factors, he let me know that I was healthier than most people who were much younger. Many questions later, we decided that I would proceed with race number ten. I recovered from that race and decided to proceed with the next event that would be held in California.

Race number eleven was America's Finest City Half Marathon in San Diego on August 18, 2013. I had decided, with the advice of my doctor, that I would keep my heart rate under a particular number to ensure that I wouldn't put any undue stress on myself or the baby. On race day, I couldn't believe how great it felt to be standing at the Cabrillo National Monument, enjoying a spectacular view as the sun rose over the starting line. Even though I was running solo that day, I had a comforting feeling from the knowledge that I had this little peanut growing inside of me. I asked someone to take a photo of me before the race so that I could someday show my child that they ran a half marathon with me before they were ever born. I look at that photo now and it brings back so many memories of this particular race, as well as the emotions that were flooding through my mind. Pretty soon after crossing the starting line, I knew that it was going to be a slow jog for me. In order to keep my heart rate low, I had to regulate my pace and breathing. At first, I felt frustrated by the slower pace, but soon relaxed as I began to pray for contentment in the situation. For the entire race, I continually brought my thoughts back to the blessing that God had given us in our miracle baby. That kept my focus and perspective in check.

At the end of the race, Rick and our children were waiting for me. I was so happy to see that I wasn't the very last runner as I had been in race number ten. My family and I sat on a sunny patch of grass and I recounted some of my memories from the day as we enjoyed a few post-race bananas. I felt good about finishing and I was thankful that I completed the race without any issues. As soon as we pulled away from the finish line area, it was time for our family vacation to begin. We had registered our children for surf lessons in Pacific Beach. It was also going to be a birthday week for my son Peyton, so we were ready for some fun. The beach was up next on our family's agenda. On Monday, surf school started and we all settled into "beach life". What a way to relax as a family!

The next day was Tuesday, August 20. I will never forget this date. I woke up just before sunrise to an odd sensation in my lower belly. At first I thought I was dreaming, but then realized that I was peeing in the bed. In just a matter of seconds, my mind raced through embarrassment to fear as the thought of my water breaking jolted me out of bed. As soon as my feet hit the floor, I heard a "splash" as something ran down my legs faster than I could catch it with the lower half of my gown. I tried to control the flow, but couldn't. I raced to the bathroom which was just a few steps away. However, the sound of liquid squishing under my feet sent my blood pressure through the roof. I tried calling to Rick as I entered the bathroom, but my voice wouldn't come. I flipped on the light switch to see that it wasn't urine that was pouring out of my body. It was blood. My lower half was now covered in it. I literally felt time stand still as I looked down to see the crimson color washing over my feet onto the floor. Again, I tried to call for Rick, but couldn't. I made it over to the toilet as I tried to catch my breath. I was now hyperventilating and feeling light-headed. My body began to shake and I was sobbing as I tried to wake Rick without disturbing our children. At this point, Graesen and Peyton had no idea that I was even pregnant. I couldn't let them find out by seeing me completely undone and covered with blood.

Finally, I managed to make enough noise to wake Rick. As he rushed into the bathroom, his face changed to something I had never seen before. He kept asking what he could do to help. He was scared. We both were. There was blood everywhere and it was still flooding out of me into the toilet. I squeezed my eyes shut so that I wouldn't see anything that would haunt me later when I thought about the precious life that was being taken away from us in that very moment. The thoughts in my head started to pour out of my mouth as I cried over and over again, "This is my fault. I did this. I killed our baby." Rick was trying to calm me down and determine what he could do. I knew that we had lost our child. That's all I could think of until my mind went into survival mode. As I sat there, I started making a list of what we should do next. I needed to get in the shower. Rick needed to find carpet cleaner and old towels to clean up the blood before our children woke up. As I stood in the shower, I started repeating the same phrases that I had earlier. But now, they were inside my head and torturing me with an excruciating sense of guilt and shame. Even though there were only two other people close to us who knew about the pregnancy, I lamented the fact that Rick and I would always know that I had killed our baby by chasing after my goal of twelve races in twelve months. How would we ever deal with that fact?

I stood in the shower for a very long time as Rick had to run out for the cleaning supplies we needed. When he returned, he found me sitting in the tub with the shower water still pouring over my head. I couldn't get up and I didn't even want to make eye contact with him. How would he ever forgive me for this? I apologized over and over again, in hopes that he would not blame me for the miscarriage. Ironically, that's exactly what I was doing. I was blaming myself. Our discussion went from sobs over our loss to my list of things we had to do to keep this from our children. He wanted to go to the hospital, but I had experienced enough miscarriages to know that there was no more baby. I couldn't face yet another doctor's visit where they matter-of-factly inform me that I miscarried, tell me to go home to rest and watch for fever or excessive bleeding. I had been through it enough to know that there was nothing anyone could do at this point to help us. Our baby was gone and I was to blame. At that particular moment, I wanted to die as well. Rick helped me out of the shower and I was shocked by what I saw in the mirror. I had lost so much blood in such a short time that my reflection was ghost white. I had dark circles under my eyes that looked as though I had been in a fight. The sight of myself in the mirror made everything worse. I saw failure, pain and fear looking back at me. Rick did his best to console me, but all I could do was slump over on the floor and sob.

Eventually, Rick was able to help me get dressed so that we could wake the children and take them to surf school. We told them that I wasn't feeling well as we drove to the beach for their lessons. I sat in the front seat, with my head down as tears poured into my lap. How could God have allowed or caused this to happen? Why did I choose to do that race? Why didn't Rick stop me? Why didn't my doctor say something to deter me from continuing my race challenge? I was trying to place my anger and blame wherever I could to stop the throbbing pain in my chest. Nothing was worth losing our miracle baby. No goal. No challenge. No race. Nothing. My heart ached and I hurt all over. I wanted to sleep, but my mind was racing. How would I ever survive the feelings that were overwhelming my mind? I tried to focus on the sound of my children's voices and their happy chatter coming from the backseat. I wanted desperately for the morning's events to be a bad dream. After we dropped the kids off at camp, we walked over to a bench that overlooked the ocean to sit and rest. I was barely moving and kept thinking that I was going to faint. My low blood pressure was an obvious problem. As we sat there, we tried to talk about what had happened. Rick reassured me that he didn't blame me, but I couldn't believe him. We tried to pray, but our words were drowned out by our sobs. My anger began to rise up and I questioned why God would allow us to get this far in the pregnancy and then take our child away. What could we possibly learn from such pain? Why did it have to happen to us? This was our miracle child.

The rest of our day was spent cleaning sheets, carpet, floors and the bathroom. I wasn't much help in the process as I couldn't move very quickly without feeling faint. I stayed as close as I could to Rick as he cleaned up any last proof that our child ever existed. In this moment, I was reminded of what an incredible gift I was given the day that God chose Rick to be my husband. He loved and served, even in times of his own grief and sorrow. The remainder of our week was odd. We did our best to put up a good front so that our children and others wouldn't suspect that anything was wrong. I had texted the only two friends who knew that I was pregnant because I was certain that they would be praying for us. I felt some comfort from knowing that they would keep us in their prayers. However, when Rick and I were alone, we cried and also prayed for mercy from the pain we were feeling. I couldn't sleep, so I would sit up and stare at the TV to pass the time. As each day passed, I started to sense all of my "pregnancy feelings" dissipate. I wasn't craving pickles any longer. The warmth in my belly was gone. I felt empty inside and there was nothing I could do to rewind time and go back to the way I had felt only days earlier.

At the end of the week, it was time to return to Arizona. I began to feel even more anxiety about going back home. I literally begged Rick not to make me go. For some reason, I felt that leaving San Diego meant that I was leaving our child. Also, I didn't want to return to all the reminders that would be waiting for me once we got back. From my first doctor's visit, I had an appointment of some kind each week. Because of my "advanced maternal age", I had more tests, bloodwork and ultrasounds than usual. I had the printed images of our baby as well as the cd and other paperwork at home. I didn't want to see those things. They would be just another reminder that I had exchanged my child's life to run a race. The guilt was consuming me and we hadn't even loaded the car for the return trip home yet. Eventually, Rick convinced me to get into the car and we made the long drive back to Arizona while I cried silent tears. My shirt was soaked and I was miserable the entire way. Sometimes my sobs would escape from my mouth in an odd-sounding gulp. Each time it happened, Rick would quickly grab my hand and squeeze it as a reminder that he was right there with me, just as he had been for more than a decade since we first met.

As we entered our house, I tried to go about my normal routine of unpacking. I noticed that we had a voice mail message, so I played it as I was putting things away. I was again struck with a combination of sadness, grief and guilt as I listened to a message from my doctor's office. The nurse had called to let me know the results of the maternity bloodwork that I had done before we left for San Diego. The tears once again started to flow. The next day, I decided to call my doctor's office to let them know of the miscarriage. Secretly, I was hoping that some of the genetic testing results would provide a reason for the miscarriage. I thought that maybe I would be freed from some of the guilt I was experiencing if there was an actual medical reason for the loss of our baby. Before I could ask any specific questions, the nurse proceeded to tell me that all the test results were great. She explained that the bloodwork showed that our baby was genetically healthy and fine. Next, she asked me if I would like to know the baby's gender. My response was simple and to the point. "You can tell me the gender, but I had a miscarriage last week." She was surprised to hear what I said and she started to ask questions to determine what might have happened. After I gave her the details, she insisted that something wasn't adding up and that she would like for me to go in for an ultrasound. She wanted to ensure that it was a "complete" miscarriage and hopefully find out what might have caused it. She even hinted that I might not have lost the baby, based on the information I gave her. That one statement wrecked me. I was now dealing with a mixture of blind hope and dire helplessness. I knew what I had seen on that dreadful morning and there was no way that our baby survived such massive bleeding. However, I agreed to go in the next day for the ultrasound. Then, I decided to enlist the help of some mighty prayer warriors. I emailed my staff team at Redemption Gateway to explain that I had been pregnant for thirteen weeks, had experienced a miscarriage in San Diego, but now had a glimmer of hope that the baby survived. Imagine getting all of that information in one email. They all responded with encouragement and biblical wisdom that I truly appreciated. To know that they were praying for us gave me a deep sense of peace, regardless of whatever may happen the next morning. It was days later when I learned that the pastors had gathered together that morning to pray specifically for our family and for the baby that may or may not have still been alive.

There aren't words to express how it made me feel to learn that they did such a selfless thing for us.

On the morning of my appointment, I went to the doctor's office alone. In his heart, Rick knew that the baby hadn't survived. He had witnessed the miscarriage and had done most of the cleaning alone. He didn't need a doctor to confirm what he already knew. At this point, I was okay with the fact that I was there alone. I had grieved to the point where a simple confirmation of the miscarriage wasn't going to send me over the edge. When I entered the ultrasound room, I explained the details of what had happened to the technician as she turned on the machine. As soon as the screen lit up, I saw movement on it. My first assumption was that this was from a previous ultrasound that was done before our vacation. When she said, "There she is. Your baby is fine", I thought I was imagining her words. I couldn't take in what she was saying as truth. I asked her if that was an old scan and she reassured me that the baby was moving because she was still alive and doing well. The sound that proceeded out of my mouth then was an odd combination of a scream, cry and laughter. I couldn't bring myself to believe what she was telling me. With that, she started to point out all the parts of my daughter on the screen. She emphasized that her little hands were folded right in front of her face, as if she was praying. My response was that she was indeed praying for her mom who was obviously insane. After more tears and more laughter, I realized that I needed to let Rick know that our daughter was still alive. I took a photo of the ultrasound picture and texted it to him, as well as my friend, Faith. I saved that text in my phone as a reminder of God's grace to me.

The next step was to meet with my doctor to find out exactly what had happened. Apparently, I had experienced a sub-chorionic hemorrhage, which is a very common thing in pregnancy. I had never heard of it prior to this. The doctor explained that most women will have minor bleeding that will form a clot and then dissolve. His assumption was that mine did not clot properly which caused the excessive bleeding to occur. He told me to rest for two weeks to give the clot that was found on the ultrasound time to dissolve. After that,

I would be free to resume normal activities. Obviously, this brought to mind the fact that race number twelve was still on my schedule. I decided that I would discuss it with Rick and make a decision about whether or not to run it after we had time to pray and seek God's will. I had two weeks of rest and I planned to follow the doctor's orders exactly as I was told. Later that day, we decided to tell our children about their baby sister. We then realized that we should probably tell others because our children might beat us to the punch if we didn't. I posted the ultrasound photo on Facebook and then sat back to watch the responses roll in about it. Most people thought that my account had been hacked. Others just posted things like "Wow!" and "What?" It was so funny to read their reactions and then respond to the questions that were inevitable.

As the time passed, Rick and I both grew more confident in the fact that I was meant to participate in the final race of my challenge, even if it meant that I would walk it. When the doctor confirmed that the clot had dissolved and that I could get back to normal activities, I asked about the race. He let me know that many women have had the same type of hemorrhage that I did, without ever running a day in their adult lives. He told me several stories of others who went through this and they never did anything close to exercise during their pregnancies. Without realizing it, he gave me some sense of peace that my actions had not necessarily caused the severe bleeding that occurred. I'm so thankful for him and the way that he cared for me during my pregnancy.

I still have many questions about why God would allow or cause this to happen in my life. I will probably never know the answers to most of them. However, I can definitely say that my trust in His plan was grown tremendously through this set of painful circumstances. I had no other choice than to trust that He was doing what was best for my good and His glory. I know that He saved my baby for a purpose, if nothing more than to give me one more child that is biologically mine. The trust that I feel for God's plan is now a part of everything I do. It gives me the strength to choose faith over fear in countless situations that have occurred in many areas of my life.

I now know that I can continue on a path in a direction where God is leading and I can trust that He will continue to open doors for me. If I'm not on His chosen path, those doors won't open. I can rest in that fact. I trust Him.

In ministry, I have always been somewhat unsure about my abilities. I know that I have skills in the area of administration. However, that can actually be a weakness when I put those tasks above the need to meet with others and share what Christ has done in my life. I feel that my past, especially my childhood, has held me back because I don't always feel worthy of counseling others. Over the past several years, I have noticed that God is growing my desire to meet with people about their struggles. I'm learning that I have something to share with others that may help them to grow their trust in God's plan for their life. As a matter of fact, I have already had the opportunity to share my perceived miscarriage with other women who have had the same type of hemorrhage. I have been able to explain the details of what happened and then assure them that my daughter was in no way affected by what took place. God gave me that story so that I could pass it along to others who might experience the same. Even with all my flaws and failures, I have something to give. It's the wisdom that I've gained from surviving situations that would cripple some people emotionally if they didn't have faith in Christ. Fortunately, God chose to save me and give me a voice to help others understand that He can make all things new, even for people like me. I trust Him and I believe that he has a plan for you too.

In my business, I have to continually choose to trust the Lord for guidance. In network marketing, so much of the business is dealing with personal development and taking control of my emotions. I have a long way to go in this area, but I can definitely see growth in my knowledge of how to share my products and business opportunity. I have been able to see God's hand in many of my meetings, presentations and interactions with other network marketing professionals. I don't see it as a coincidence or luck that I joined this profession in 2012. I see it as God putting me exactly in the place that He wanted me to be so that I could grow as a person and as a business woman. He is teaching me how to bless others through my business, not to bless my business through others. I love being able to look back and see the ways that He has moved me through this process. During those times when I waiver in my faith and start to allow fear back in, I can trust that He will hear my prayers for discernment and that He will answer them. I am enjoying all that I have the privilege of doing as I build my business and share the journey with others who are doing the same.

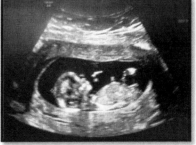

Family at the finish line ... there's nothing better.
Race #11 – America's Finest City Half Marathon
August 2013

A fun finish to a challenging twelve months.
Race #12 – P.F. Chang's Rock 'n' Roll Half Marathon
September 2013

Lesson #12:

Enjoy Your Victory Lap

Have you ever watched a NASCAR race when the winner takes their victory lap? It's definitely a fun thing to watch, even if you aren't a racing fan. The joy on their faces is undeniable once the checkered flag waves. They slow down the car as they take it around the track one last time. Sometimes, they even take it for a slippery spin on the grass. I've even seen a driver turn a back flip off the window frame of their car. It's a celebration for everyone who has the chance to witness it. Many times when I see the "victory dances" of athletes, sports teams and others, I try to reflect on all the hard work that it took for them to realize their dreams of achieving their particular goal. I try to imagine what they had to endure or experience in order to be victorious. I ponder the thought of how many hours they had to invest in training and preparing for their win. I know that behind every great finish line celebration is a story of big dreams, hard work, perseverance and faith.

When I chose race number twelve, there were several factors to consider. I wanted to have a larger race venue so that there would be more support on the route. I knew that, because of my pregnancy, it would take me a lot longer. I wanted a place that would have cooler temperatures. I also wanted someone to share it with me that I could trust to stop me from going too far in any way that could harm me or my baby. I was still very cautious about completing this final race, even though I had been cleared medically. I definitely didn't want to go through the experience alone, so I asked my best girlfriend to join me for my victory lap. Faith blessed me when she agreed to do the race with me. She joked that she would be able to keep up with me since I was pregnant. Faith is a pro at encouraging others. I can always depend on her to have my best interest at heart, and to be bold enough to keep me in line when I need it. She stood next to me as I married Rick in 2003. She was with me for the births of my first two children. She cried and prayed with me when I believed that I had suffered a miscarriage several weeks earlier after race number eleven.

For me, the victory lap started long before I crossed the finish line of race number twelve which was the P.F. Chang's Rock 'n' Roll Half Marathon in Providence, Rhode Island on September 29, 2013. While I was looking for my final race, I had noticed that my company was hosting one of its signature personal development seminars in Hartford, Connecticut on the same weekend. I knew that I had to check the surrounding areas for a possible race. It was then that I found the half marathon event in Providence. As we planned for the trip, we decided to make it a fun weekend. We would spend time in Boston with some of my husband's family and visit friends of mine in western Massachusetts. We would then drive over to Hartford so that I could express my gratitude to my company's founder for teaching me the power of the "I Am" statements that had led to this race challenge. I also wanted to be certain to thank my friend, Jordan, whose teaching was invaluable as I learned from him how I could succeed in business as well as my goal to be a marathon mom.

As I made arrangements for my travel, I could already see God's hands at work in the plans. My friend, Betty, had offered me two more airline passes for the final race of the challenge. What a blessing it was to have her offer such incredible gifts to me for the first and last race. She will always hold a special place in my heart for her generosity that provided the "bookends" of my race challenge. Getting to the finish line was not going to be an easy task for the last race. Traveling on airline passes was a bit tricky. Faith and I made it to Denver and hoped to catch a flight from there to Boston. When it seemed that we might not make it to Boston, we decided to take a break for lunch. While walking to the gate to wait for the next flight, who should we meet, but Betty? She was working that day and was on her way back east to go home. We quickly latched onto her and asked for help on how to get to Boston. We followed her lead and eventually arrived in Massachusetts much later than we had originally planned.

The next day, Faith and I decided to see the city of Boston together. I had been there several times prior, but it was different seeing the sights with Faith. We walked and laughed and ate. We met people, asked them to share their stories with us and then ate some more. We met firemen, got lost and then found a small Italian restaurant for some more good food. We obviously had the excuse that we were carb loading for our upcoming race, so that seemed to make it okay. The next day, we drove out to visit my friends, the Normans, in Ashburnham. We celebrated their anniversary with a nice dinner and some great conversation. I was thrilled to be back in New England. It was a perfect time of the year to be there and I was enjoying all the great memories that were running through my mind as I spent time in an area with people that I loved so dearly.

On Saturday, we drove to Hartford so that I could deliver some cards and gifts of gratitude to the men who had taught me to dream big again and then go after those dreams with focused intensity. My plan was simply to give them the gifts, express my appreciation for the way that they had impacted my life and then head over to Providence to pick up our race packets. I gave Jordan his gift and asked if he could pass along the other one to the company's founder after the seminar. Jordan asked if I could stay for a moment and share my story during the "I Am" portion of the event. I was surprised at the request, but felt so blessed to have the opportunity to thank both of these men publicly for what they had taught me. I was able to share what I had learned, how it had led to my race challenge and then how I would be completing the final race on Sunday morning. The feeling of a "full circle moment" became a reality for me. Being able to end such a challenging and rewarding twelve months in this way was something that could only come from God.

As we left the seminar, Faith and I realized that we were going to have to move fast in order to reach Providence before the race expo closed. If we didn't arrive by 5:00pm, we wouldn't be able to retrieve our packets and run the race on Sunday. There was lots of nervous laughter on the trip over to Rhode Island as I did my best to stay somewhere close to the speed limit, but still arrive on time. As we watched the miles roll by, we also watched our gas gauge begin to approach the empty mark on the dashboard. Our jokes turned to tense anticipation that we might not make it to the expo. If we stopped for gas, we would certainly lose valuable time. If we didn't stop for gas, we might not make it all the way to the location where we had to pick up our packets. We both felt some relief when we realized that we were less than a mile away from our destination.

At that moment, my heart sank when I felt the steering wheel lock up and the engine die as the empty gas tank took its toll. I had just a few seconds to get the car almost completely out of the lane before everything shut down. I was devastated. After all this time and planning, I was going to miss my final race. With just minutes before the expo was going to close, Faith grabbed my ID and hers, and took off running down the sidewalk. She told me to find a way to get gas and that she was going to get our packets, no matter what. Before I could absorb what was happening, she was out of sight, literally. I found myself standing next to our rental car, looking at my pregnant reflection in the store front window that faced the street. I wasn't sure what I could do next, but I figured that someone had to be around that could help us. I walked up and down the street, trying to find any business that was open. Unfortunately, there was none to be found on that late Saturday afternoon. The area seemed almost deserted. My mind raced with the fact that Faith would most likely not be able to retrieve my race packet. There were strict rules against that with this particular race organizer. I was alone in a town that I didn't know and feeling like a beached whale on the side of the road.

About that time, people started to pour onto the sidewalk. From the look of all the jerseys that they were wearing, it was some sort of sporting event that had just ended. Later, I found out that the Providence Bruins had just finished a pre-season hockey game. As I stood on the sidewalk, hoping that someone would take pity on me, I was met with people who just wanted to give me directions to the closest gas station. Somehow they missed the fact that I didn't have a car to get there. When I started to feel completely abandoned, I caught a glimpse of something that is now engrained in my memory.

Faith came jogging up the hill, waving a couple of plastic bags and a red gas can over her head. As she got closer, I could see that she was smiling also. A wave of relief washed over me as she breathlessly recounted how she convinced the race organizers to let her pick up my packet. She had let them know that I was a pregnant woman who was, at that point, standing on the sidewalk trying to find a way to get gas for our car. Next she detailed how she had bought the gas can from a security guard at the convention center where the expo was being held. I laughed at the thought of her running around trying to put everything together so that I could finish my race challenge and enjoy the feeling of victory. I then cried at the thought of all that she had just gone through to make it happen. A true friend can be hard to find, but to have one who will go to great lengths for someone else's dreams...well, that's almost impossible.

What she did next was simply crazy. We finally found a man who offered to give us a ride to the gas station. Faith volunteered to be the one to go while I stayed with the car. As soon as the guy pulled up in his van, I felt an uneasy feeling in the pit of my stomach. It was an older van with all the seats pulled out of it. Faith didn't seem to notice when she hopped into the front seat and waved as they pulled away. I immediately took down his tag number, just in case. I started to pray for her safety and then realized that our families would kill us both if they knew what we were doing as she drove away with a complete stranger. As I waited, I tried to keep track of time in my head because my phone had long since died. Leave it to me to forget to bring my charger. To my relief, Faith returned about fifteen minutes later with gas in her newly purchased red can. The guy didn't offer to help with the gas, so Faith and I stood on the side of the road and filled the tank as we whispered and giggled about the events of the past hour. She then let me know that the "kidnapping van" had scared her as well. One of us mentioned that it would be a great story to tell in a book someday. Ironically, I had not thought of or planned to write a book about the challenge at that time.

After a trip to the gas station for a complete fill-up, we were off to have dinner with my husband's family. Uncle John and Aunt

Rosa were the perfect hosts. We were also blessed to have several members of the family join us. Cousins Danny and Clara were in town from New York. It was great to catch up and spend time with both of them, Cousin Nelly, and her son, Daniel. Uncle Luis and Aunt Janet were there too. They came with their own unique sense of humor and some delicious food. Together, the family had prepared a feast that was fit for a king. It was a great evening, full of laughter, as we recounted the details from our adventurous day. Sharing our stories and being cared for by family was the perfect way to prepare for the final leg of my challenge. We ate well, laughed a lot and experienced the support and encouragement of everyone there.

At the end of the evening, Uncle Luis gave us a personal escort to his family's condominium that was just a few miles from the starting line of what would be my final race. I was thankful that he was taking us there because I certainly didn't want to have any more unexpected adventures that night. Once we got settled into the condo, Faith and I discussed the final details before climbing into bed. However, just moments after our heads hit the pillows, a ridiculous sounding horn blared so loudly that we both jumped up to see what it was. Eventually, we determined that it was some sort of fog horn to keep the boats safe on the water that was flowing right in front of the complex where we were staying. The horn was so loud that we could clearly hear it, even with the windows shut. For the rest of the night, it would go off about every fifteen minutes. We giggled hysterically every time it blared, until we both crashed from exhaustion.

The next morning, we woke up feeling a bit groggy, but super excited for whatever the day would hold. We got ready, took photos, went through our pre-race routine and then headed downtown to the starting line. We were there in just a few minutes. Everything went surprisingly well. As I walked around and enjoyed the atmosphere with Faith, I knew that God had put this final race together in a way that I could enjoy as I reflected back on what He had done over the past year. I was able to share some of my experiences and feelings with Faith that morning that I most likely would not have shared with others. Even my fears and thoughts of inadequacy were met with compassion and encouragement from Faith. She has always known what to say to me. That fact was never more obvious than on this particular day.

As we made our way into the starting line corrals, my heart began to race. My mind started to flash back through my previous races, similar to a scene in a movie. I remembered my first race in San Jose with Rick there to love and support me. I recalled the second race when I realized that my running was going to leave an impact on my children, both foster and biological. I had experienced victory with my young daughter as she completed her first running event during my third race. I thought about Cynthia and the way that she had put in her own mileage to encourage me during my races in San Diego. I smiled when I thought about Laura and Logan who spent the weekend in San Francisco with me for the seventh race. I thought about Lorin, Rachel and the others who supported me through my tenth race when I was incredibly sick from being pregnant. I saw Rick in San Diego, holding my hand and comforting me when I felt overwhelming grief. Ultrasound images, doctor's appointments and the faces of so many people who had supported me during the challenge were scrolling through my thoughts. Then I looked over at Faith and became very emotional as I knew that God had provided exactly the people that I needed in my life to complete such a phenomenal journey. He knew exactly when and where to place each person who had been a part of my story for the last twelve months. It was about that time that I was jolted out of my stroll down memory lane when I realized that the starting line announcer was looking at me and asking about the shirt I was wearing. It said, "12th Race in 12 Twelve Months...Baby's 3rd in Three". He asked me to turn around so that everyone could see it which caused some cheers and applause to erupt around me. I couldn't have asked for a better way to start my final race of the challenge.

Once we got started, it wasn't long before I knew that we would be doing a "turtle trot" that day. It didn't bother me at all, except for the fact that we had to keep stopping at each set of porta potties along the route. We took our time on the course, enjoying every step of the way. We engaged in several conversations with people who noticed my shirt and asked how I was doing. We talked about ways that we had seen God work throughout my challenge. We reminisced about the days leading up to this particular race and we laughed, a lot! The miles seemed to roll by without incident and I began to feel excitement as I could hear the cheers from the finish line area. As we turned into the chute, we agreed to finish strong. The tears started rolling down my face and I'm certain that I had the "ugly cry" going on as I felt the joy of victory come within my grasp. For some odd reason, as I stepped across the finish line, I decided to wipe my feet on the mat that was used to cover the timing wires. It wasn't a planned action, but it sure felt good. It appeared as if I was trying to scrape something off of the bottom of my shoes. Then, someone on the sidelines noticed what I was doing. A guy shouted out, "You go girl! Finish that race! You did good! Woo Hoo!" His high-pitched voice, squeals of laughter and applause that followed were just icing on the cake. I couldn't have said it better myself. This was my victory lap, but others were along for the ride. That made it even more important for me to finish strong.

I was overjoyed and breathless at the thought of actually being able to finish the final race. I reflected on the fact that God had carried me every step of the way for the previous twelve months. In times of joy, as well as times of pain, His plan was unfolding in my life. He grew me in ways that I am still discovering. His unconditional love was there, even when I had a hard time accepting it. I was blessed. I was grateful. I was speechless. Those few moments at the end of the race, which marked the completion of my self-imposed challenge, gave me a symbolic glimpse of what I will get to enjoy one day in heaven. After a long and tiring journey, I will get to hear these words from the Lord, "Well done, good and faithful servant!" It will be a time when I will get to celebrate all that He has done in my life, in His presence. Until then, I will continue to trust in His plan for my life, here and now. My hope and prayer is that because of this challenge and all that I learned throughout it, I will always choose faith over fear. I want others to see that if I can do these things in Christ, anyone can.

Cool Down, Stretch and Reflect

At the end of each of my races, I always took time to relax in the finish line area. I gave myself a chance to unwind and cool down from the miles I had just run. I worked through a set of stretches that helped my body recover and ultimately prepare for the next challenge. I also seized the opportunity to take stock in what had happened that day and appreciate everything that it took for me to accomplish my goal. At the end of this race challenge, I was encouraged to have a similar type of finish line routine by writing this book. I look back on this particular twelve months in time and see many instances where God was at work in my life. Because of this year of intentional running, I see a puzzle that He slowly and precisely put together for my good and His glory. I can see it in each of my races, but in different ways. I see it in the people that took the journey with me. My trust in the Lord grew immensely as I was forced to rely on His strength in a variety of situations. I was also blessed to see how He was giving me the desires of my heart and teaching me to share my blessings with others.

For example, my initial plan was to run my first race in November 2012 in Phoenix. However, as the weeks passed, I started to feel anxious and wanted to get started sooner. I knew that there had to be a good race somewhere in October, so I went to several race websites to see what I could find. That's when I found the P.F. Chang's Rock 'n' Roll Half Marathon in San Jose. For some reason, when I saw the words San Jose, I thought it was in Texas. I know. I was a geographically challenged homeschool mom. I wasn't sure how easy it would be for me to get a flight into Texas and run my first race of the challenge alone. Fortunately, my husband Rick (aka Rickquest) enlightened me by letting me know that San Jose is in California. Duh! When he informed me that it was close to San Francisco, I felt my heart skip a beat. It was one of those many times when I quietly whispered, "Okay, God. What are you doing in this?" I immediately thought of something else that I had listed on my original "I Am" page back in June. At that time, I had written the letters "RSF" for Redemption San Francisco in the margin of my paper. I didn't have any specific thing in mind to write about this church. I just wrote those three letters and nothing more. Until the moment when we were discussing San Jose, I wasn't even sure why I had written it. It was random and out of context for me to even be thinking about that church. I knew the pastor, Justin, who left Arizona to plant it, but that was about it. He and I had never had more than a two minute conversation. Imagine my surprise when I realized that I would be within driving distance of his home when I ran my first race of the challenge. God was doing something. I just wasn't sure what that was at the time. That's no longer the case. While in San Jose for race number one, we were able to meet with Justin, find out about the church and determine ways that we could be a source of support and encouragement to them. It made my first race extra special when I saw how the Lord had put me there for something more than just running. I love it when God puts the pieces together in such a perfect way.

Also, I've been able to reflect back now and see how the Lord placed me in the network marketing profession at exactly the right moment when I would need to focus on personal development and growth. The concept of gratitude was one that I had never really thought about on any deep level. However, through my company, I was able to learn more about it and actually put it into action as a way to love and serve others. I grew deeper in my faith and ultimately closer to the Lord as I chose to focus on His blessings, as well as the people He had placed in my life. Over the years, I have been able to help others to experience some of the same benefits that I enjoy by living a grateful life with intention.

As I finish this book, I am also teaching a class on gratitude that I created with the pastors and elders of our church. In "Gratitude: The Missing Link", we explore gratitude as the key to unlock the purpose for which God created each of us, which is to be a conduit of His blessing to His world. Without being introduced to my network marketing company, I wouldn't have had the experience to even think about teaching others how they too can bless others through appreciation. I think back on the past three and a half years of my life and it's easy to see how God was putting all of these events in place for me to be a part of something pretty incredible in our church.

I also believe that I was being prepared for the pain and grief that would come as we experienced the reunification of our foster sons with their biological family. Like most people who consider the idea of being a foster parent, we weren't sure how we would feel if any of our foster children would return home to the family that initially could not care for them. By discussing this with other foster parents, we eventually realized that reunification is the ideal situation when God mends a family and puts them back together. We wanted to minister to the entire family and not just the children, whenever possible. However, when it came time for us to say goodbye to our boys, the grief was incredibly difficult to handle.

By spending time in a company with other people who continually challenged me to focus on the positive things in life, I was able to redirect my grief and sadness by turning my eyes to the Lord and seeing what He was doing in the midst of the pain. Much of the teaching that I was experiencing in network marketing could be applied to my role as a foster parent. I was learning how to grow personally and also help others. I was challenged to intentionally live a life of gratitude and avoid negativity whenever possible. Obviously, there are a lot of negative influences when dealing with the child welfare system. However, we were able to rise above much of the "noise" that would consume a lot of our time. Rick and I saw it in ourselves as individuals, as well as our family. Sometimes we would even remind each other in difficult times, "Rise above the noise. Rise above." We used it along with scripture to keep one another accountable and on track with the mission and purpose that God had given us as foster parents. As we grew in our faith and let it override our fears, we also noticed that circumstances which had paralyzed us previously no longer had a hold on us. Where once we would spend time worrying and being anxious about a particular situation, we could now walk through it confidently and move on in the direction we knew would best benefit the children in our care.

As I've taken the time to recall many of the events from my race challenge, I can also see how God was giving me courage with each victory I experienced. I know that I am not always the most confident and bold version of myself that I can be. However, I can look back over the last several years and see that fear has no place in my life. It is crippling and holds me back from experiencing true joy. It imprisons and often kills dreams as it takes control of my thoughts and emotions. I know that I'm not alone in this battle with fear and anxiety. That's why I chose to share my story so that others can rest in knowing that it is possible to win once we firmly commit to choosing faith over fear.

I pray that you will begin to think about your own story. Don't allow what has happened in your past, or even what is happening in your present, hold you back from your future. Rest in knowing that your story can and will bless others. Step out in faith to let others know about your journey. Ask for help. Make a difference by sharing what God has done in your life. Conquer any fear you have in this process with a faith that surpasses human understanding.

Whether your goal is to run a race, plant a church, become a foster parent, start a business or rid yourself of debt, I encourage you to pay attention to what God might be doing to prepare you for such a challenge. Whatever your dream may be, my prayer for you is that you will place your trust in Him to clear the path before you. Do this as you pray for discernment and ask for the Lord's help. Focus on your goals, no matter what they are, and realize your wildest dreams. In Christ, you can do all things.

May God bless you so that you can be a blessing to others.

I'll see you at the finish line!

Therefore, since we are surrounded by so great a cloud of witnesses, let us also lay aside every weight, and sin which clings so closely, and let us run with endurance the race that is set before us, looking to Jesus, the founder and perfecter of our faith, who for the joy that was set before him endured the cross, despising the shame, and is seated at the right hand of the throne of God.

Hebrews 12:1-2

TOO TOUGH TO KILL

At mile 20, I thought I was dead.

At mile 22, I wished I was dead.

At mile 24, I knew I was dead.

At mile 26.2, I realized I had become too tough to kill.

-Author Unknown

Race #2 – Lady Speed Stick Women's Half Marathon
November 2012

Hot Chocolate 15K – No Medals Here!
December 2012

My Favorite Way to
Carb Load:
Hot chocolate and
muffins!

Race #4 – P. F. Chang's Rock 'n' Roll Marathon
January 2013

Life on Planet Marrs = Faith Over Fear!

About the Author

Ellen was born in northeast Georgia, the middle child of three. Before her twelfth birthday, she had already experienced more loss, trauma and grief than most adults. After the passing of her birth mother to cancer, Ellen's stepfather decided that he no longer wanted to be responsible for her. Fortunately, her aunt and uncle made the decision to raise Ellen after she was literally dropped off at their home with no place else to go.

Despite the painful details of her early years, Ellen refuses to allow the circumstances of her past to define her. She fuels her passion to help others and make a difference in the world by sharing her story with abuse victims, foster children and potential foster parents. As a speaker, trainer and mentor, she motivates and inspires others to overcome difficult circumstances, pursue their dreams and achieve their goals with unbridled passion.

In 2011, she and her husband, Rick became licensed foster parents. In that role, they were blessed to have six children come into their lives and capture their hearts. In 2014, the Marrs family grew from four people to nine with the adoption of a sibling group from foster care and the birth of their daughter, Jaeden.

Ellen spends her time working in ministry at Redemption Gateway church, homeschooling her children, training for marathons and mentoring potential foster and adoptive families. She also teaches individuals, businesses, entrepreneurs and non-profit organizations the importance of expressing gratitude. She does this through her network marketing business, as well as her class, "Gratitude: The Missing Link". To relax, she enjoys running, riding motorcycles and spending as much time as possible outdoors with her family.

Ellen, Rick and their seven children currently reside in Gilbert, Arizona. If you'd like to learn more about the Marrs family, check out their blog at lifeonplanetmarrs.com.

Connect with Ellen:

www.ellenmarrs.com

www.marrscards.com

facebook.com/ellen.marrs.3

instagram.com/ellenmarrs

twitter.com/EllenMarrs

info@ellenmarrs.com

Recommended Reading

As you'll notice, my reading list is a mixture of Christian, business, network marketing, and inspirational influences. These books have all contributed something positive to my life in the last several years. I wanted to share them with you, in hopes that you'll be inspired as well.

The Four Year Career, Richard Bliss Brooke

Promptings, Kody Bateman

Beach Money, Jordan Adler

Go Pro, Eric Worre

The Principle of the Path, Andy Stanley

Yes, Sometimes It Is About the Money, Steve Schulz

Mach II with Your Hair on Fire, Richard Bliss Brooke

Stay the Course, Adam Packard

MLM Blueprint, Kody Bateman

I Like Giving, Brad Formsma

The Treasure Principle, Randy Alcorn

RockStar System for Success, Craig Duswalt

More Than Enough, Dave Ramsey

You Can Change, Tim Chester

What's Best Next, Matt Perman

Jab, Jab, Jab, Right Hook, Gary Vaynerchuk

EntreLeadership, Dave Ramsey

Managing God's Money, Randy Alcorn

One Thousand Gifts, Ann Voskamp

Choosing Gratitude, Nancy Leigh DeMoss

Why Didn't Someone Tell Me This?, Natasha Duswalt

The Total Money Makeover, Dave Ramsey

The Grace and Truth Paradox, Randy Alcorn

Next Generation Leader, Andy Stanley

Made in the USA
Middletown, DE
26 July 2018